The CHEW
WHAT'S FOR DINNER?

ALSO AVAILABLE FROM *The Chew*

The *New York Times* Bestselling

The Chew: Food. Life. Fun.

100 EASY RECIPES for EVERY NIGHT of the Week

The CHEW
WHAT'S FOR DINNER?

Edited by PETER KAMINSKY and ASHLEY ARCHER

HYPERION
NEW YORK

CONTENT COORDINATOR
Kerry McConnell

FOOD
Photographer: Andrew Scrivani
Prop stylist: Francine Matalon-Degni
Food stylists: Martha Tinkler
Jackie Rothong
Ian McNulty
Lauren Palmeri
Crafter: Tom Tamborello

CRAFTS
Photographer: James Ogle
Crafters: Tracy Kleeman, Adrienne Henry, Michael Buckholtz, Jamie Smith
Hand model: Ai Takami

The Chew: What's for Dinner?—Photographer Credits:
Donna Svennevik/ABC: 15, 50, 69, 108, 111, 127, 129, 151, 189, 205, 206, 208, 209; Fred Lee/ABC: 97, 139; Heidi Gutman/ABC: 123, 117; Ida Mae Astute/ABC: 107, 135; James Ogle/The Chew: 1, 9, 25, 30, 38, 39, 43, 77, 79, 93, 95, 163, 177, 215, crafts on 130, 131, 146, 147, 148, 149, 226, 227; Lorenzo Bevilaqua/ABC: 84, 99; Lou Rocco/ABC: vii, 10, 19, 27, 29, 33, 41, 53, 63, 71, 115, 121, 133, 143, 173, 221, 223, 233

Book design by Vertigo Design NYC

Library of Congress Cataloging-in-Publication Data
The Chew, what's for dinner? : food, life, fun / edited by Peter Kaminsky and Ashley Archer. — First edition.
pages cm
Includes bibliographical references and index.
ISBN 978-1-4013-1281-7 (alkaline paper)
1. Cooking, American. 2. Dinners and dining--United States. 3. Chew (Television program)
I. Kaminsky, Peter. II. Archer, Ashley. III. Chew (Television program) IV. Title: Chew.
TX715.C529 2013
641.5973—dc23
2013010164

ISBN: 978-1-4013-1281-7

FIRST EDITION

3 5 7 9 10 8 6 4

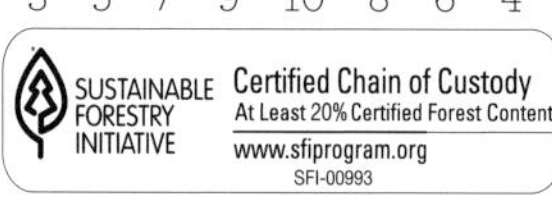

THIS LABEL APPLIES TO TEXT STOCK

We try to produce the most beautiful books possible, and we are also extremely concerned about the impact of our manufacturing process on the forests of the world and the environment as a whole. Accordingly, we've made sure that all of the paper we use has been certified as coming from forests that are managed, to ensure the protection of the people and wildlife dependent upon them.

This book is dedicated to all of the talented, hard-working people who make up the creative, production, and technical staff of *The Chew*. They give their best every day and we love them for it.

CONTENTS

The
CHEW

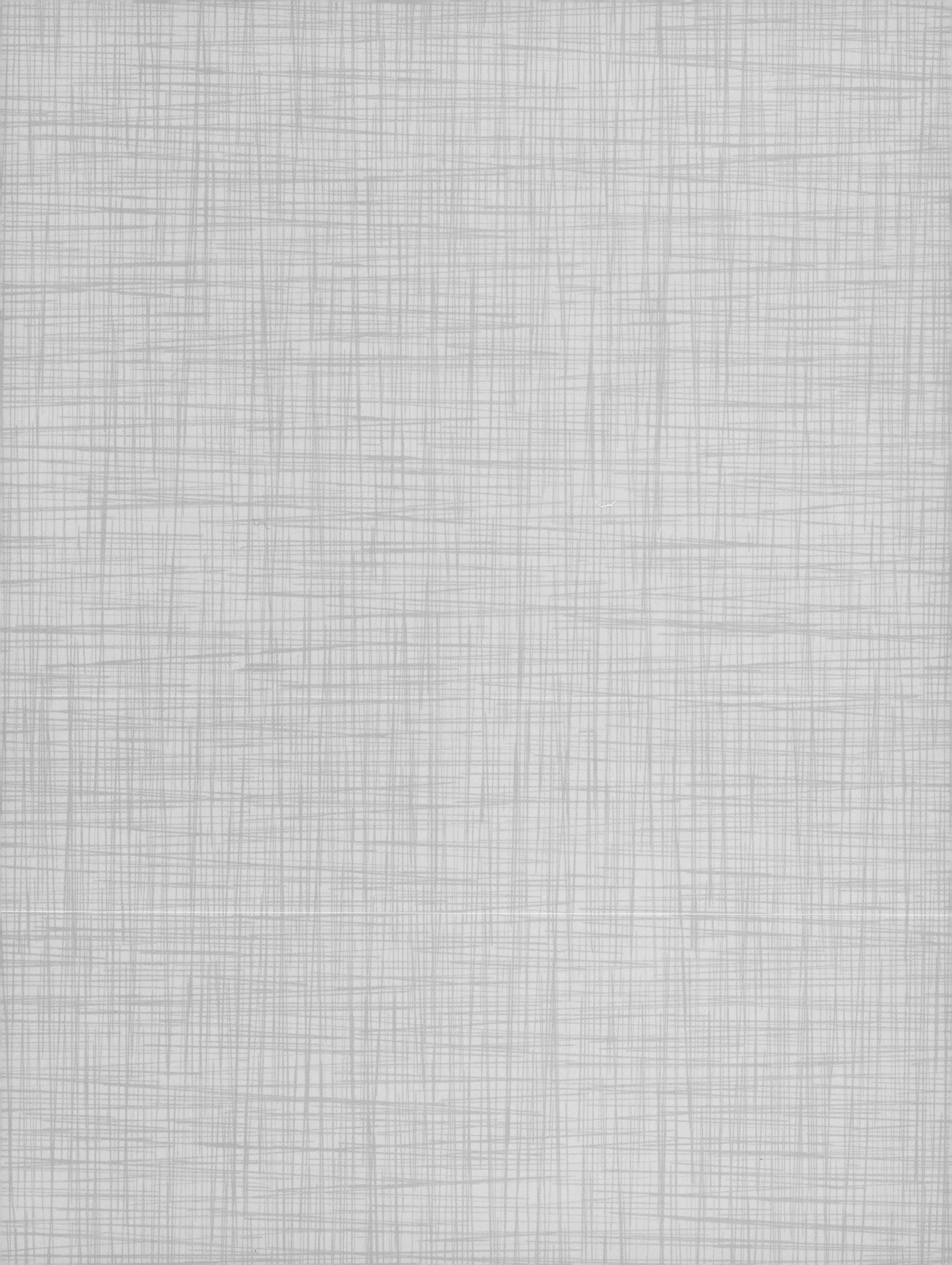

INTRODUCTION

If *The Chew* has done nothing else, I hope it's shown that home cooking shouldn't feel like math, it should feel like finger painting. A splash of wine into this, a little extra butter into that, a squeeze of lemon over these . . . yeah, baby!

Every day I stand in front of the studio monitors and watch *The Chew* as an excited fan. I groove on the beautiful food and the laughs as these easy friends pull a meal together in a few minutes. They inspire me by making it look fun. And useful.

As a below-average cook with above-average ambition, I imagine myself making whatever delicious dish they're making that weekend or, if it's stunningly easy, that night.

It's a seduction of sorts, like this book. Ever since we started the show we have wanted people to swap the stressful idea of "making dinner" for the fun of creating something new for themselves and their family.

If we did it right, this book should have something for every possible kind of home cook, every day of the week.

We also built this book around the rhythm of people's lives. Weekdays are often rushed, but weekends shouldn't be. And if we are cooking for special occasions, we want to show love through care and time spent.

So we put a little fancy weekend stuff like Lobster Thermidor (see page 191), some simple midweek yummies like Chicken Marsala (page 48), the perfect dish for date night, and a recipe for Sunday dinner that will stand the test of time.

As we say on the show, we hope our recipes are just the start. Don't be afraid to get finger painting and make them your own work of delicious art.

—Gordon Elliott

IT'S MONDAY!

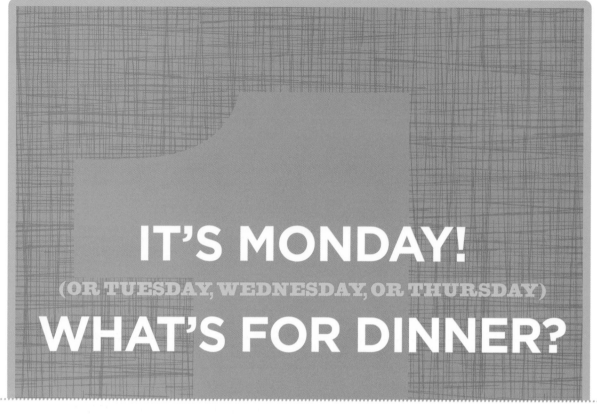

(OR TUESDAY, WEDNESDAY, OR THURSDAY)

WHAT'S FOR DINNER?

QUICK AND EASY MEALS TO MAKE ON BUSY WEEKNIGHTS

BREAKFAST + DINNER = "BRINNER!"

SWEET TREATS FOR THE MIDDLE OF THE WEEK

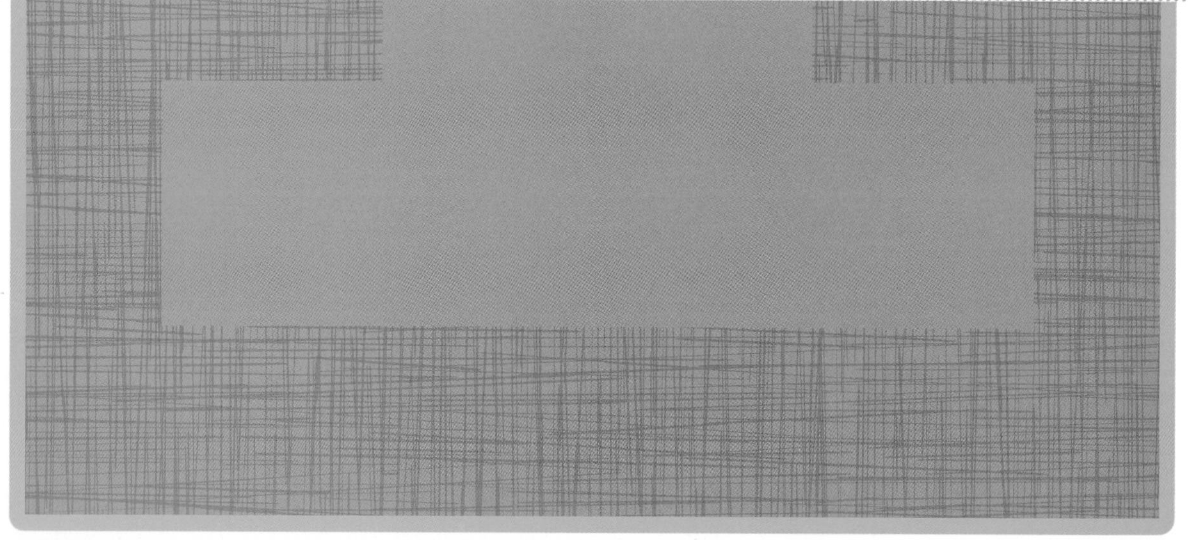

“**ON THE CHEW,** we think everyone should cook, because everyone has it within them to do it well. The problem is weeknights. How do you find the time? The recipes that follow are proof positive that you can make simple and delicious meals any night of the week with just a few ingredients from your pantry and a little bit of shopping. **THE PAYOFF IS HUGE.** Homemade food is more nutritious; contains less fat, salt, and chemicals than most store-bought stuff; and tastes better. Sure you could order in a pizza or open up a can of soup and throw it over a chicken breast, but it is so much more fulfilling and healthful to cook a meal with the best-tasting natural ingredients. If there is another person who likes to cook or help in your family, it's that much easier and that much more quality family time. Who doesn't like to sit down to a home-cooked meal with the family? For many of us, it's the only time of the day we get to **DO SOMETHING TOGETHER** and that is very precious. And speaking of precious, did I mention that it's cheaper too?

“But I can't cook,” you say. To which I say, yes, you can, and these recipes will prove it. Whether you start at the age of eight or twenty-eight or forty-eight, you've got to start somewhere. Don't worry if it's not perfect. **WHO NEEDS PERFECT?** You just need good, and our Chew Crew promises these easy meals are good. Just get in there and do it. Pretty soon you will be **FREAKIN' AWESOME** as a home cook. And speaking of awesome home cooks, here are some thoughts on Monday through Thursday home cooking from my partners on *The Chew.*”

—Clinton

SALAMI AND EGG SANDWICH | CHORIZO MANCHEGO STRATA | CHILLED TOMATO AND BREAD SOUP | GRILLED SHRIMP WITH GRAPEFRUIT SALAD | ZUCCHINI CRUDO | GINGER ALE CARROTS | GRILLED APRICOT AND RADICCHIO SALAD | CHEESE RAVIOLI WITH GARLIC, MUSHROOM, AND ROSEMARY SAUCE | PASTA FAGIOLI | KIELBASA AND BEAN STEW | LOBSTER ROLL | SHOESTRING FRIES | CAPRESE SANDWICHES | PATTY MELT | ONION RINGS | SPICY SAUSAGE SLIDERS | ANGEL HAIR CAPRESE | SEARED SCALLOPS WITH RAISINS, PISTACHIO, AND SPINACH | SPAGHETTI WITH GREEN TOMATOES | CHILI SALMON WITH MANGO CUCUMBER SALSA | ANGEL HAIR WITH OLIVE OIL, GARLIC, AND CHILI FLAKES | LEFTOVER NOODLE PANCAKE WITH FALL FRUIT SLAW | GRILLED CHICKEN THIGHS WITH WATERMELON FETA SALAD | GRILLED CHICKEN CLUB | CHICKEN MARSALA | CHICKEN SALTIMBOCCA WITH CAPERS AND GRAPEFRUIT | HOT SAUCE FRIED CHICKEN | DORM ROOM CHICKEN CHILI | 60-SECOND GUACAMOLE | GRILLED SKIRT STEAK WITH CAULIFLOWER HASH | GRILLED SKIRT STEAK SANDWICH WITH CHARRED CORN MUSTARD | PAN-SEARED STRIP STEAK WITH MUSHROOMS AND CARAMELIZED ONIONS | PORK TENDERLOIN SCALLOPINI | OZ FAMILY FRIED RICE |

QUICK AND EASY MEALS TO MAKE ON BUSY WEEKNIGHTS

I'M A LITTLE BIT of a creature of habit. Liz and I eat a lot of pasta during the week, always with a great salad. In summer I like a rib eye and a Greek salad. I think to cook well, quickly, and with low stress, there isn't enough that can be said about how important it is to build your pantry: good spices, vinegars, olive oils, canned tomatoes, anchovies, canned beans—things that aren't perishable. I shop from a rough list, but I never actually follow it—most of the time I see something in the store that really gets me excited and start building from there. That's kind of our Monday through Thursday plan.

—Michael

GOOD DOESN'T MEAN A BIG PRODUCTION. On a weeknight, we're usually talking just a course or two. At the supermarket, I check out what's on special or if something looks particularly good. When it's farmers' market day, you can't beat that. Then there's my pantry. I keep good tomato sauce, beans, lentils, split peas, inexpensive balsamic (that I reduce by about half), extra virgin olive oil, spicy spices (like chipotle flakes, chili powder, or pimento), and homemade bread crumbs (dark golden brown).

What do I make out of all this? Many, many things, but I guess my go-to easy dishes are roasted chicken legs and thighs with paprika and balsamic glaze; spaghetti with garlic, oil, and chili flakes, sprinkled with toasted bread crumbs; a big green salad with white beans, eggplant Parmesan, and celery root; sweet potato hash with sunny-side up eggs; white bean, lentil, or split pea soup with (to jazz it up) arepas or johnny cakes with polenta, or quick whole grain drop biscuits. Nothing takes more than ten minutes or so of prep and very little standing over the stove.

—Mario

"**PEOPLE SAY THEY DON'T HAVE THE TIME,** but take one day and log how you spend every single chunk of 10 minutes and you will quickly see how much time goes to checking your phone or Facebook or other nonessentials. If you can find a way to consolidate 15–20 minutes of that time, you can make a home-cooked meal. What I focus on is my pantry, fridge, and freezer, stocked with the things that I know my taste buds rely on for satisfaction. I'll always have canned beans and dry pasta. I eat a ton of quinoa. For breakfast I'll do a hot grain cereal with coconut milk and maple syrup. I keep lettuce on hand because I'm big on making the easy choice the healthy choice. If salad fixings are the first thing I see when I open the fridge, I'm probably going to go for it. But I like to spice up my salads, so I usually have hard fruits like apples and pears that won't go bad quickly. In my freezer, I have my glazes, sauces, stocks, and frozen herbs: ingredients that I can just add to a pot that instantly flavor it up."

—Daphne

"**FIRST THE SHOPPING**—I will look in my cabinet and see what I have, and then go shopping with a loose list that I can adjust if something in the store catches my fancy. I always start with produce—that's what dictates the rest—then dairy, and then meat, and we do a lot of pasta. I'm one of those people who loves meatloaf and seeing what I can make work with the meat and vegetables I have on hand. A lot of times my husband and I will do what we call abundant salads: we chop a medley of veggies together on our big cutting board. If we have some leftover meat, that goes in too. And then there's grits—I'll throw anything into grits. I just did some this past weekend with butternut squash and herbs. But they have to be good grits. I'm lucky that way; I get great grits from Tennessee. Gotta be white grits too, no exceptions."

Salami and Egg Sandwich

SERVES 4 | COOK TIME: 4 MINUTES | PREP TIME: 15 MINUTES | COST: $

Easy

Around my house my mom was the master cook, but my dad was "the Sandwich King." If I had to pick a favorite—and that's not easy—I'd probably have to say nothing beat his salami and eggs. Something fantastic happens to salami when you fry it—you get a crispy crust, almost like bacon. Then with some Hungarian ShaSha Sauce (basically hot mustard and hot pepper), compliments of Lizzie's mom, and sliced pickled onion, you have a full-frontal attack on your taste buds.

4 egg knot rolls or potato rolls

2 tablespoons unsalted butter

1 pound salami, thinly sliced

2 tablespoons extra virgin olive oil

4 eggs

1 cup spicy mustard or ShaSha Sauce (recipe follows)

1 cup thinly sliced or Pickled Red Onions (recipe follows)

1 bunch basil (leaves only)

Kosher salt

Freshly ground black pepper

1. Preheat a griddle or nonstick skillet to medium-high heat.

2. Split the rolls, and butter each half. Place on the griddle and toast until browned. Set aside.

3. Put the salami on the griddle in four separate mounds and warm through, allowing some pieces to crisp.

4. Using the olive oil to grease the griddle as needed, fry each of the eggs, about 1 minute per side for over easy. Assemble the sandwiches by spreading spicy mustard or ShaSha Sauce on each of the buns, adding the salami, topping with the sliced or Pickled Red Onions and basil leaves, and finishing with a fried egg. Season with salt and pepper and place the bun on top and enjoy.

FOR THE SHASHA SAUCE

12 hot banana peppers from a jar, tops removed and chopped

4 cloves garlic

1 cup yellow mustard

1 cup white wine vinegar

½ cup sugar

2 tablespoons all-purpose flour

TO MAKE THE SHASHA SAUCE

1. In a food processor, puree the peppers, garlic, mustard, and vinegar.

2. Pour the puree into a medium saucepan, then add the sugar and bring it to a boil over high heat. Lower the heat and simmer the mixture for 30 minutes.

3. In a small bowl or juice glass, mix the flour and ½ cup water to make a smooth paste. Whisk it into the pepper mixture and continue to simmer for 20 minutes, stirring regularly, until it becomes very thick. Let the sauce cool, and then pour it into a covered nonreactive container (such as a glass jar). The sauce can be refrigerated for up to 1 month. Makes 2 cups.

FOR THE PICKLED RED ONIONS

2 pounds red onions, sliced

White wine vinegar (amount will vary for each jar)

Sugar (amount will vary for each jar)

Kosher salt (amount will vary for each jar)

2 teaspoons mustard seeds

1 tablespoon crushed red pepper flakes

2 tablespoons coriander seeds

2 tablespoons black peppercorns

4 cloves garlic

2 bay leaves

TO MAKE THE PICKLED RED ONIONS

1. Pack the onions into two 1-quart jars and cover with water to come within ½ inch of the rim. Pour the water out into a measuring cup. Note the volume, pour off half the water, and replace with the vinegar. Add 2 tablespoons sugar and 2 tablespoons salt for every 3 cups of liquid.

2. Pour the vinegar mixture into a nonreactive saucepan. Add the mustard seeds, red pepper flakes, coriander seeds, black peppercorns, garlic, and bay leaves, and bring to a boil over high heat. Allow the liquid to boil for 2 minutes, and then remove it from the heat.

3. Pour the hot liquid into the jars to cover the onions and screw on the lids. Refrigerate for up to 1 month.

4. Makes: 2 quarts

Chorizo Manchego Strata

SERVES 8 | COOK TIME: 40–50 MINUTES | PREP TIME: 15 MINUTES | COST: $

Easy

I've yet to meet the person who doesn't like bread pudding. For breakfast—maybe with a splash of maple syrup and a bunch of raisins staring at you from its eggy, breadful depths—it's hard to beat. Now, if you make it savory you've got a quick dinner that comes together without much fuss. There are two kinds of chorizo that you are apt to find in America. The hard kind is from Spain and is already cooked. The softer kind is from Mexico and is more suited for a hash than this recipe. But fear not, admirers of things Mexicano, I top off my strata with a very Mexican tomatillo salsa. You can probably make this with any hard cheese that has good meltability, but if you can, go with the original from La Mancha in Spain: gotta go Manchego.

8 cups crusty sourdough bread, preferably day-old

2 tablespoons extra virgin olive oil

1 large onion, chopped

1 pound Spanish chorizo, medium dice

2 cloves garlic, peeled and sliced

12 eggs, whisked

1½ cups milk

1½ cups half-and-half

1 tablespoon red chili flakes

2 cups Manchego cheese, shredded

Kosher salt

Freshly ground black pepper

Store-bought tomatillo salsa, to serve

1. Preheat the oven to 375 °F.
2. Cut the bread into 1-inch cubes, and set aside.
3. In a large sauté pan, heat the olive oil over medium-high heat. Add the onion and sauté for 2–3 minutes until soft. Lower the heat to medium and add the chorizo. After 2 minutes add the garlic and cook just until fragrant, then set aside to cool.
4. Whisk together the eggs, milk, half-and-half, chili flakes, and 1½ cups of cheese, and season with salt and pepper. Add the bread and chorizo mixture to the eggs and toss to coat. Press down firmly to coat all of the bread in the egg mixture. Pour into a greased baking dish. (At this point you could cover and refrigerate overnight.)
5. Bake for 35–40 minutes uncovered, then let stand for 5–10 minutes. Grate the remaining cheese over the top, and serve with tomatillo salsa.

Chilled Tomato and Bread Soup

SERVES 8 | COOK TIME: 2 MINUTES | PREP TIME: 20 MINUTES

INACTIVE COOK TIME: 1 HOUR TO OVERNIGHT | COST: $

Easy

Opera fans in Italy have been known to throw rotten tomatoes onstage when they are not pleased with the performance. Before you aim a tomato because of a poorly sung aria, make sure you are not heaving almost-rotten tomatoes, because super-ripe, over-the-hill tomatoes are the basis of one of the favorite quick summertime meals in my home. Toss them into a food processor with day-old bread, salt, herbs, and olive oil, and you have a real Tuscan bread soup. It's flavorful and healthful, so we always keep a big container of it in the part of the refrigerator where we store the stuff we call "Kids Can Eat as Much as They Want, Whenever They Want."

5 pounds very ripe heirloom tomatoes, cored and cut into chunks

3 cups torn-up day-old Italian or country bread

½ cup fresh basil leaves

2 tablespoons fresh thyme leaves

Kosher salt

Freshly ground pepper

¼ cup extra virgin olive oil

Zest and juice of 2 lemons

2 teaspoons red pepper flakes

4 scallions (whites and about 2 inches of greens), thinly sliced

8 ½-inch-thick baguette slices, toasted

1. In a food processor or blender, blend the tomatoes until smooth. Add the day-old bread, basil, and thyme, and season with salt and pepper. Blend. If too thick, thin with water. Refrigerate for at least 1 hour to chill, but it's even better the next day.

2. In a medium mixing bowl, gently mix the olive oil, lemon zest and juice, red pepper flakes, and scallions together. Season lightly with salt.

3. Divide the chilled tomato soup among eight bowls. Float 1 slice of toast in the center of each bowl. Sprinkle the scallion mixture on top of each toast, and serve.

Grilled Shrimp with Grapefruit Salad

SERVES 4 | COOK TIME: 18–20 MINUTES | PREP TIME: 20 MINUTES | COST: $

Easy

For our Mother's Day show, I wanted to do something bright, light, and flavorful instead of a big ol' hunk of meat like you'd do for Father's Day, so I came up with this fresh and delicious salad. One of our audience members, Hakim Chandler, volunteered to help me whip it up and said that he would make this recipe for his "soon-to-be-pregnant wife." I thought that might be a little too much information about the Chandler household, but he quickly corrected himself: "My soon-to-be-a-mother wife." Whew!

This is a twist on a classic Middle Eastern tabbouleh salad of bulgur wheat and fresh herbs with my additions of grapefruit sections, lemon zest, and, of course, good olive oil. Hakim was a little challenged in the lemon-zesting department until Carla, revealing another one of her hidden talents, told him to "hold the lemon like you are throwing a knuckleball!"

He did fine in the lemon-holding department and behind the stove. We agreed that this would be a great recipe to whip up for Mom while she is busy with their new baby.

FOR THE SALAD

2 cups water

½ cup bulgur wheat, rinsed

½ teaspoon kosher salt

Zest and juice of 3 lemons

½ cup extra virgin olive oil

3 cups flat-leaf parsley, chopped

¼ cup scallions, chopped

½ cup mint leaves, chopped

3 grapefruits, segmented and cut into thirds

TO MAKE THE SALAD

1. Bring the water to a boil. Add the bulgur, reduce to a simmer, and cook until the bulgur has absorbed all the water and is slightly tender, about 12 minutes. Season with the salt, and set aside to cool.

2. In a small bowl, whisk together the lemon zest and juice and olive oil.

3. In a large salad bowl, combine the parsley, scallions, mint, and grapefruit. Add the bulgur, pour the dressing over the salad, and toss to combine. Taste and adjust for seasoning. You might need to add more salt or olive oil. If you need more olive oil, add it 1 tablespoon at a time. Set aside until ready to serve.

FOR THE SHRIMP

12 jumbo shrimp, peeled and deveined

2 tablespoons olive oil

Kosher salt, to taste

Freshly ground pepper, to taste

TO MAKE THE SHRIMP

4. In a medium bowl, toss the shrimp lightly with the olive oil, salt, and freshly ground pepper.

5. Preheat a grill pan to medium-high heat. Grill the shrimp for 3–4 minutes per side, until the shrimp are pink and cooked through.

6. Divide the tabbouleh into four servings, and place 3 shrimp on each of the salads to serve.

Zucchini Crudo

SERVES 4 | PREP TIME: 10 MINUTES | INACTIVE PREP TIME: 10–15 MINUTES | COST: $

Easy

If you have a garden, then you know that you can save time "shopping" because it doesn't require anything more than going out the back door and picking whatever is ripe. You also know that when you have zucchini, you really have lots of zucchini. No big deal, because this fresh summertime salad goes with just about anything you might make, from grilled salmon to pork chops, from steak to lobster. Remember to salt your zucchini slices ahead of time, so that you remove some of the water and any bitterness. A simple lemon shallot vinaigrette brightens the flavors beautifully.

- 2 medium zucchini, thinly sliced
- 2 medium yellow summer squashes, thinly sliced
- 1 tablespoon plus ¼ teaspoon kosher salt
- 1 teaspoon garlic, peeled and minced
- 1 shallot, peeled and finely sliced
- Zest and juice of 3 lemons
- ½ cup extra virgin olive oil
- ⅓ cup slivered or sliced almonds, toasted
- ⅓ cup fresh dill, chopped

1. Combine the zucchini and yellow squash in a colander in the sink, and sprinkle 1 tablespoon of the salt over it. Toss to coat, and set aside for 10–15 minutes, no longer.

2. In a large bowl, combine the garlic and shallot, sprinkle with the remaining ¼ teaspoon salt, and whisk in the lemon zest and juice. Whisk in the olive oil in a steady stream, then the almonds and dill. Taste for seasoning and acidity (it should be nicely acidic). Add the zucchini and squash to the dressing, toss, and serve immediately.

Use your fingers

The ingredients in any vinaigrette vary a lot—one lemon is super sour, another not so much; olive oil can be soft and floral, or sharp and peppery. To make sure you have the right balance, dip the tip of your finger and taste. Your tongue won't lie.

Ginger Ale Carrots

SERVES 4 | **COOK TIME: 15–20 MINUTES** | **PREP TIME: 10 MINUTES** | **COST: $**

Easy

I like this longtime Christmas favorite so much, and it's so quick, easy, and flavorful, I decided, why not make it on a weeknight? It will add some amazing flavors and textures alongside your main course. It's spicy, sweet, fruity, and fresh-tasting.

Carla stood by my side when I was making this and said it could work for lots of different vegetables. I haven't tried it yet, but I bet she's right. Cauliflower for sure. Maybe delicata squash. I'm not sold on the idea of broccoli, but if it floats your boat, give it a try and let me know.

1½ pounds young carrots, peeled, with greens trimmed (leave about 1 inch of the green tops on)

4–5 tablespoons olive oil

Salt

Freshly cracked black pepper

Zest and juice of 2 oranges, divided

2 cloves garlic, smashed

½ cup ginger ale

1 tablespoon ginger, finely minced

¼ cup chopped hazelnuts, toasted

¼ cup chopped parsley, divided

1. Preheat the oven to 400 °F.
2. In a large bowl, toss the carrots with the olive oil and season generously with salt and pepper. Add the zest and juice of 1 orange and the garlic cloves, and toss to coat.
3. Heat a large ovenproof sauté pan over medium-high heat. Arrange the carrots in an even layer. Pour in the ginger ale and cook the carrots on the stovetop until they begin to color, and then transfer to the oven and cook for about 10–15 minutes, or until fork-tender.
4. Once the carrots are cooked and the glaze has reduced, remove from the oven and allow to cool slightly.
5. Meanwhile, in a small bowl, mix together the remaining orange zest and juice, ginger, hazelnuts, and parsley. Season with salt and pepper. Garnish the carrots with the hazelnut mixture.

Grilled Apricot and Radicchio Salad

SERVES 4 | COOK TIME: 8–10 MINUTES | PREP TIME: 15 MINUTES | COST: $

Moderate

Grilling season is also ripe fruit season. One of my favorite sides for grilled steak is apricots tossed in a marinade and then grilled. The savory aspects of the marinade help tie the fruitiness of the apricots to the meat. You can certainly do this over a gas grill, but wood charcoal gives a certain extra quality of smoky char that is indescribable. You don't need to do this with apricots only. Any stone fruit will do the trick: peaches, plums, nectarines. It really presents the jewels of summer orchards in a new and great-tasting way.

1 shallot, minced

3 tablespoons red wine vinegar

1 tablespoon honey (chestnut if you can find it)

1 bunch mint (leaves only)

3 tablespoons extra virgin olive oil

Kosher salt

½ pound apricots, halved and pitted

1 head radicchio, quartered, with core intact

1 cup feta, crumbled

1. Preheat a grill or grill pan to medium-high heat.
2. In a mixing bowl combine the shallot, red wine vinegar, honey, mint, and 2 tablespoons of the olive oil. Whisk together and season with salt. Add the apricots and radicchio to the bowl, and toss to coat in the dressing.
3. Place the apricots and radicchio, cut side down, on the grill. Cook for 3 minutes, until they are slightly charred and have caramelized. Flip the radicchio and cook for 3 more minutes. Remove the apricots and add them to the bowl with the mint dressing.
4. Remove the radicchio from the grill and thinly slice. Add the radicchio and the feta to the bowl with the apricots, and toss to combine. Adjust seasoning and serve warm.

Cheese Ravioli with Garlic, Mushroom, and Rosemary Sauce

SERVES 6 | COOK TIME: 8–10 MINUTES | PREP TIME: 10 MINUTES | COST: $

Easy

Attention ravioli lovers! Did you know you can enjoy ravioli just as much without tomato sauce, especially if you make this quick and super savory garlic, mushroom, and rosemary sauce? Once you boil the ravioli, put them in the pan with the other ingredients and add a little of that starchy pasta water, and in about a minute, you will have a beautiful, clean-tasting, fresh pan sauce. I like to throw a little pat of butter in mine, which Mario says isn't truly Italian. But the way I look at it, although I'm Sicilian and Greek, which makes me an olive oil kind of guy, I was trained in a French kitchen where the motto was "It's better with butter!"

Kosher salt

4 tablespoons butter

2 tablespoons olive oil

2 sprigs rosemary

2 cups cremini mushrooms, cleaned and sliced

Freshly ground black pepper

1½ pounds store-bought cheese ravioli (fresh or dried)

4 cloves garlic, peeled and thinly sliced

1 large shallot, peeled and minced

⅓ cup Parmigiano-Reggiano, plus more for garnish

1. Heat a large pot of boiling water over high heat and season generously with salt.

2. Heat a sauté pan over medium-high heat. Add 2 tablespoons of the butter and the olive oil. Once hot, add the rosemary sprigs and mushrooms. Toss the mushrooms and season with salt and pepper. Cook until the mushrooms have browned on all sides, about 5–6 minutes.

3. Meanwhile, drop the ravioli in the boiling water and stir with a wooden spoon, cooking 1–2 minutes less than the package instructions suggest.

4. Add the garlic and shallot to the mushrooms, and toss to coat. Cook 2–3 minutes, or until the garlic and shallot are soft.

5. Drain the ravioli, reserving some of the pasta water, and add the pasta to the sauté pan and toss to coat. Add about ⅓ cup of the pasta water, along with the remaining 2 tablespoons of butter. Add the Parmigiano-Reggiano, and toss the pasta until the sauce is creamy and emulsified. Serve immediately, garnished with more Parmigiano-Reggiano if you want.

Pasta Fagioli

SERVES 6 TO 8 | COOK TIME: 30–35 MINUTES | PREP TIME: 15 MINUTES | COST: $

Easy

Pasta fagioli! Say it with me: pasta *fah-joe-lee.* Damn, that's a fun word. The trick to making it quickly—and even though I'm a big shot Italian TV chef, I use this trick—is to buy canned beans. Molto fast, molto easy. Take note that it calls for tomato paste, not crushed tomatoes. When you add tomato paste to the onions and the hot oil, the flavor deepens and intensifies. I make it with pancetta, but chicken works as well; or, for you vegetarians, seitan or tofu. When I have leftover pasta dough, I always toss it into soups like this, but dried pasta is just as good. In fact, this is one of those recipes where almost anything you think to add is fine.

3 tablespoons pancetta, diced

6 tablespoons extra virgin olive oil

¼ cup Italian parsley, finely chopped, plus more for garnish

1 medium Spanish onion, finely chopped

2 tablespoons tomato paste

8 cups chicken stock

3 cups cooked borlotti beans or kidney beans (rinsed and drained if canned)

2 cups fresh pasta scraps or broken dried fettuccine

Kosher salt

Freshly ground black pepper

Grated Parmigiano-Reggiano, for garnish

1. In a Dutch oven, heat the pancetta and 2 tablespoons of the olive oil over high heat until almost smoking. Add the parsley and onion, and cook, stirring, until the onion is browned and soft, about 5 minutes.

2. Stir in the tomato paste, reduce the heat to medium, and cook for 5 more minutes. Add the chicken stock and beans, and bring to a boil. Lower the heat and simmer for 10–15 minutes.

3. Add the pasta, and simmer for 6–8 more minutes if using fresh, and according to package instructions if using dried. Remove from the heat, and season with salt and pepper.

4. Divide the soup among six serving bowls. Drizzle with the remaining olive oil, and garnish with the parsley and grated Parmigiano-Reggiano to serve.

Herbed up

When I cook a recipe like this with herbs, I like to put some in at the beginning so that it infuses the dish with a muted low-end flavor. Then I add some fresh herbs at the end to bring out those high notes.

Kielbasa and Bean Stew

SERVES 6 TO 8 | COOK TIME: 35–40 MINUTES | PREP TIME: 10 MINUTES | COST: $

Easy

When winter hangs in the heartland like an uninvited guest who won't go away, you want something hearty on your plate. That's when I turn to the undisputed king of sausages, the pride of Poland, the smoky, salty kielbasa. Stewed with sauerkraut, braised in beer, and cut with some sharp mustard greens, this is just the thing to whip up after an overtime shift at the auto plant or on any cold night when the walk from the car to the front door makes you pray for spring. This won't set the dogwoods blooming, but it'll surely warm you up.

2 tablespoons butter

1 yellow onion, sliced

Salt

2 tablespoons olive oil

1 pound kielbasa sausage, chopped

2 carrots, peeled and sliced into coins

1 tablespoon mustard seed

1 12-ounce stout beer

½ pound Yukon Gold potatoes, halved

1 bunch mustard greens or kale, stems removed and thinly sliced

2 cups sauerkraut, drained

2 cups chicken stock

3 tablespoons fresh parsley, chopped

1. In a large Dutch oven, add the butter, onion, and a pinch of salt. Cook on low until the onions have caramelized, about 10 minutes. Transfer the caramelized onions to a bowl and set aside.

2. In the same pan, add the olive oil and turn the heat to medium-high. Add the sausage and brown for 1–2 minutes. Add the carrots and mustard seed and cook for 5 more minutes. Deglaze the pot with the beer. Add the potatoes, mustard greens or kale, and sauerkraut to the Dutch oven, along with the caramelized onions.

3. Add the chicken stock and parsley to the pot, and season with salt. Cook for 20 minutes until the potatoes are cooked through.

Lobster Roll

SERVES 4 | COOK TIME: 2 MINUTES | PREP TIME: 20 MINUTES | COST: $$

Easy

One of the unbreakable commandments of the Batali homestead is "Thou shalt never throw out any lobster." So if there's any leftover from Clinton's *magnifique* thermidor, my advice is to make this lobster roll. My other advice is to make your own mayonnaise. Lobster is such a noble ingredient, it wants something more than store-bought mayo. Whip up your own, preferably with the very best olive oil you can find. As for the buns, store-bought are fine; in fact, they are the only way to go, toasted, buttered, and heaped high with lobster.

1 lobster (steamed or boiled, with the meat picked out) or leftover lobster meat

1 stalk celery, small dice

½ teaspoon celery salt

¼ cup Fresh Mayo (recipe follows)

Salt, to taste

Freshly ground pepper, to taste

Butter, to brush the griddle

4 split-top hot dog rolls

1. Roughly chop the lobster meat and add to a bowl with the celery, celery salt, and Fresh Mayo. Season to taste with salt and pepper. Mix gently with a rubber spatula to combine.

2. Preheat the griddle to medium-high. Brush the griddle with butter. Toast each roll on both sides and fill with the lobster salad.

FOR THE FRESH MAYO

2 egg yolks

1 teaspoon lemon juice and zest

1 cup vegetable oil

Salt, to taste

Pepper, to taste

1 teaspoon Dijon mustard

Dashes of hot sauce, to taste

TO MAKE THE FRESH MAYO

1. In a bowl, mix the egg yolks and lemon juice and zest. Then drizzle in the oil slowly while whisking vigorously to emulsify the oil into the egg. Season with salt and pepper to taste. Add the mustard and hot sauce, and combine thoroughly. Makes 1½ to 2 cups mayo and can be stored in the fridge for up to 10 days.

NOTE: If the mayo doesn't come together or the emulsification is broken, it can be saved by putting a teaspoon of water in a fresh clean bowl and slowly whisking in the broken mayo until it recombines.

Shoestring Fries

SERVES 4 | COOK TIME: 5–10 MINUTES | PREP TIME: 15 MINUTES | COST: $

Easy

It's a shame that the only way most of us eat French fries is at a fast-food place or a restaurant. Think of all the meals you make at home that would be even more super with some hot, salty, crispy fries. Aside from a thermometer to make sure your oil is at the right temperature, there are no special chef secrets: just three ingredients and some paper towels to drain them. No recipe could be easier, or tastier.

Vegetable oil, for deep-frying

3 russet potatoes, peeled

Salt

1. Fill a Dutch oven two-thirds of the way with the vegetable oil. Heat to 360 °F.

2. Using the julienne attachment on a mandolin, cut the potatoes into strips and fry in batches until golden brown.

3. Drain the fries on a paper towel–lined plate and season with salt while they are still hot.

Caprese Sandwiches

SERVES 4 | PREP TIME: 5 MINUTES | COST: $

Easy

The English have their strawberries and cream; the French have their croissants and coffee; and we Italians have our wonderful caprese. Caprese is shorthand for the combination of fresh tomatoes, fragrant basil, and rich, creamy mozzarella, named in honor of the beautiful and idyllic isle of Capri. It really is the essence of summer, which is why I love to have caprese sandwiches when we go to the beach. One piece of advice: wait until you actually get to the beach before you assemble them, otherwise you will have soggy caprese, which is a major no-no. These sandwiches are also a Batali household go-to meal any night of the week.

1 baguette

2 pounds heirloom tomatoes

1 pound fresh mozzarella

Olive oil, to drizzle

Red wine vinegar, to drizzle

Coarse salt, to taste

Freshly ground pepper, to taste

1 bunch basil

1. Slice the baguette lengthwise.

2. Slice the heirloom tomatoes and the mozzarella into ½-inch-thick pieces.

3. Drizzle the baguette with olive oil and red wine vinegar. Layer the tomatoes and mozzarella on the bread, and season with salt and freshly ground pepper. Garnish with basil leaves, and sandwich the slices of bread together. Cut the baguette into 4 sandwiches and serve immediately.

Patty Melt

SERVES 4 | COOK TIME: 10–12 MINUTES | PREP TIME: 10 MINUTES | COST: $

Easy

A patty melt is not a burger, as any patty melt lover can tell you. The meat patty in a patty melt is all one thickness, instead of a lump that's thicker in the middle. It's also not served on a bun: you put it on rye bread with a piece of Swiss. It's important, as the juices from the meat seep into the bread, making it all gooey and delicious on the inside. When we made it on the show, Carla reminded the audience that you don't want any patty (or burger) to be much smaller than the bread (or bun) it's going on. That means you start with a patty that's just a little bit bigger than the bread, because the meat will shrink when you cook it.

- **1 pound 80/20 ground beef**
- **Salt**
- **Freshly ground pepper**
- **4 slices Swiss cheese**
- **2 tablespoons butter, plus more to brush the griddle**
- **2 tablespoons olive oil**
- **1 onion, sliced**
- **⅓ cup ketchup**
- **⅓ cup mayonnaise**
- **3 tablespoons pickle relish**
- **8 slices rye bread**

1. Preheat a griddle to medium-high heat.

2. Shape the ground beef into 4 patties. The patties should be the shape of the bread. Season generously with salt and pepper. Brush the griddle with a little butter and cook the patties on the griddle for 3–4 minutes per side, for medium rare. Top the patties with the cheese after flipping. Remove when the cheese has melted and set aside.

3. Add 2 tablespoons of the butter and the olive oil to the griddle, and add the onion. Cook until the onion has softened, about 5 minutes. Remove from the griddle and set aside.

Full steam ahead

A little trick that every short-order melt-maker (and burger-maker) knows is that you can melt a slice of cheese quickly if you put it on the patty, cover it with a lid, and give the griddle or skillet a spritz of water that instantly turns to cheese-melting-hot steam.

4. Mix together the ketchup, mayonnaise, and pickle relish.

5. Place the burger patties onto a slice of the bread. Top with some of the onions and a smear of the ketchup mixture. Top with another piece of bread.

6. Brush the griddle with more butter, and place each sandwich onto the griddle. Once the first side is golden brown and crisp, brush butter onto the top slice of bread and then flip the sandwich over. Cook for an additional 2–3 minutes until golden brown and crisp and the cheese has melted.

Onion Rings

SERVES 4 TO 6 | COOK TIME: 5–10 MINUTES | PREP TIME: 10 MINUTES | COST: $

Easy

Kids are often amazed when they find out that the onion rings they get at the burger stand can be just as good—even *better*—when you make your own batter and fry them up at home. The hardest part to this recipe is crowd control: they smell so good and look so tempting, it's hard to keep the family from snatching them just as fast as they come out of the fryer.

Vegetable oil

2 large onions, cut into ½-inch slices

1½ cups all-purpose flour

1½ teaspoons cayenne

2 teaspoons paprika

1 teaspoon kosher salt

2 eggs

1¼ cups milk, plus more if needed

2 cups panko bread crumbs

Additional salt, for seasoning

1. Fill a Dutch oven two-thirds of the way full with vegetable oil, and bring the temperature to 365 °F.
2. Separate the onion slices into rings.
3. In a medium-sized bowl, whisk together the flour, cayenne, paprika, and salt.
4. Dredge the onion rings in the flour mixture, shake off excess, and set aside.
5. Make a well in the flour mixture, add the eggs, and slowly pour in milk. Whisk until the batter has a smooth, thick consistency. Add more milk if needed. Dip floured onion rings into batter and let excess drip off. Then place rings in panko bread crumbs and thoroughly coat on both sides.
6. Working in batches, deep fry a few of the rings at a time for 1–2 minutes, or until golden brown.
7. Remove to a paper towel to drain. Season with salt immediately and serve while still hot.

Spicy Sausage Sliders

MAKES 8 SLIDERS | COOK TIME: 5 MINUTES | PREP TIME: 5 MINUTES | COST: $

Easy

Once you say the word *sausage*, you've got my attention. As a true son of the Midwest, I love sausages, whether it's brats, chorizo, merguez, or Italian sausage. One of the things I don't love about sausages is that they take a long time to cook, so for this sandwich, I take the sausage meat out of its casings and make patties. They cook a lot quicker and develop a nice crunchy crust. I love grilled onions on regular (burger) sliders, so I figured, why not here too? And then, because I'm a Greek and we love to use yogurt and mint to fill out the flavor of grilled lamb, I thought it wouldn't hurt here. As you finish one slider and reach for the next (most people do), I think you'll agree I was right.

1 tablespoon extra virgin olive oil, plus more for grilling

1½ pounds spicy sausage, removed from casing

2 red onions, sliced into ¼-inch rounds

8 mini potato rolls, split

¾ cup Greek yogurt

2 tablespoons mint, chopped

Salt

Pepper

Handful of arugula leaves

1. Preheat a grill over high heat. Brush the grill with olive oil.

2. Form the sausage into 3-ounce patties, slightly larger than the rolls. Place on the grill and cook for 2 minutes on each side. Grill the onions alongside the sausage until charred and soft, about 2 minutes per side. Toast the bread on the grill.

3. While the patties are cooking, mix together the yogurt, mint, and olive oil, and season with salt and pepper.

4. Build the sliders with sausage patties, a smear of yogurt, arugula, and grilled onions.

Angel Hair Caprese

SERVES 5 | COOK TIME: 5 MINUTES | PREP TIME: 5 MINUTES | COST: $

Easy

Lizzie and I keep a good-sized garden in the summertime, so around mid-July, there are always a lot of tomatoes on hand. If we are ever stumped as to what we should have for dinner, our garden speaks to us, often in Italian. If you listen to your garden, it might also tell you that you have some zucchini that wants to jump in the pasta bowl. Lizzie and I are all for that, but mostly we go for the basic caprese combo of tomatoes, mozzarella, and basil with some pan-roasted garlic, crunchy bread crumbs, and hot olive oil. A great thing about using angel hair pasta is that it is so thin that it cooks up quickly.

Kosher salt

1 pound angel hair pasta

¼ cup plus 2 tablespoons extra virgin olive oil

4 cloves garlic, sliced

1 pound cherry or grape tomatoes, halved

1 bunch basil, torn, plus more for garnish

1 cup bocconcini, or fresh mozzarella, cut into cubes

Freshly ground pepper

¼ cup fresh bread crumbs

2 tablespoons parsley, chopped

1 tablespoon grated Parmesan

1. Bring a large pot of water to a boil and season generously with salt.
2. Drop the angel hair into the water and cook for 1 minute less than package instructions.
3. In a large sauté pan over medium heat, add ¼ cup of the olive oil and the garlic. Sauté over low heat until the garlic becomes fragrant (being careful not to let it brown), about 3 minutes.
4. Add the cooked pasta to the olive oil and garlic with a little pasta water.
5. Combine the tomato, basil, and mozzarella in a large bowl. Season generously with salt and freshly ground pepper. Add the pasta mixture and toss.
6. In a small sauté pan, toast the bread crumbs with the remaining olive oil, parsley, and Parmesan.
7. Divide the pasta among 5 bowls, and garnish with the bread crumbs and basil.

Add taste, subtract time

I always cook pasta for 1 minute less than it advises on the package and finish it in the pan. For this recipe, I toss it in the pan with hot olive oil, garlic, and a little bit of the pasta water. That way, the pasta finishes cooking by absorbing the flavor of the oil and garlic.

Seared Scallops with Raisins, Pistachio, and Spinach

SERVES 4 | COOK TIME: 5 MINUTES | PREP TIME: 5 MINUTES | COST: $

Moderate

The single most important thing in cooking scallops is *don't overcook them*! You want 'em with a crust on one side and very rare and moist in the middle. The second piece of advice I have is once you put them in the pan *don't move them.* If you start flipping them in the pan like an overcaffeinated chef, you'll never get a crust and you'll suck all the juice out and they'll be tough and rubbery. The third thing to remember is to dry them before sautéing by putting them on a paper towel in the fridge. If you don't, they will weep a lot of liquid in the pan and you'll never get a pretty golden-brown crust. If you follow those rules, you will turn out scallops just like the ones you get in a restaurant.

Scallops are a lot like chicken: you can pretty much cook them with anything. They like sweet ingredients, tangy ingredients, savory ingredients, spicy ingredients, and don't let me forget salt. I tried all of the above in this recipe. It came together in 5 minutes, and Carla tried to eat the whole thing before she let me grab a bite. I guess that was her way of telling me it was good.

½ cup white wine

⅓ cup golden raisins

6 tablespoons olive oil

10 large scallops, patted dry, foot removed

Kosher salt

Freshly ground black pepper

⅓ cup pistachios, toasted and roughly chopped

Zest and juice of 1 orange

3 tablespoons butter

¼ cup parsley, leaves picked and chopped

10 ounces baby spinach, cleaned

1. Heat two large sauté pans over medium-high heat.
2. Heat a small sauté pan over medium-high heat, and add the wine and raisins. Bring up to a simmer and cook for 3 minutes, just to plump the raisins.
3. Add 3 tablespoons of the olive oil to one pan. Season the scallops on both sides with salt and pepper, and then place the scallops in the hot pan. Let sit for 2–3 minutes before flipping, ensuring that the scallops develop a dark golden sear. Add the pistachios and the orange juice and zest. Remove the pan from the heat and stir in the butter and parsley.
4. In another pan, add the remaining olive oil and the spinach. Season with a pinch of salt and pepper, and toss to coat a few times. Once the spinach just starts to wilt, take off the heat, about 45 seconds.
5. To serve, place the spinach on a platter and top with the scallops and sauce.

Spaghetti with Green Tomatoes

SERVES 4 TO 6 | COOK TIME: 9 MINUTES | PREP TIME: 5 MINUTES | COST: $

Easy

Clinton once asked us, "How do you satisfy a craving in your soul?" I'm pretty easy: maybe some golf on TV or Marvin Gaye on the stereo, definitely a little nap, and then a bowl of spaghetti, like this one, made with a pesto of parsley, mint, arugula, and basil stirred into fried green tomatoes. It's a perfect color for a St. Patrick's Day pasta feast, except where are you gonna find green tomatoes in March? One thing to remember is, when you quickly cook the tomatoes, don't be tossing everything around maniacally—let the tomatoes develop a little bit of a crust, then toss in your pesto for 1 or 2 minutes.

Salt

¼ cup fresh mint leaves

¼ cup fresh basil leaves

¼ cup Italian parsley leaves

¼ cup arugula, washed and spun dry

2 cloves garlic, chopped

¼ cup freshly grated Parmigiano-Reggiano, plus more for garnish

¼ cup plus 2 tablespoons extra virgin olive oil

Freshly ground black pepper

5 green tomatoes, cored and chopped

1 pound spaghetti

1. Bring 6 quarts of water to a boil in a large pot, and add 2 tablespoons of salt.

2. Meanwhile, in a food processor, combine the mint, basil, parsley, arugula, 1 clove of garlic, Parmigiano-Reggiano, and ¼ cup of olive oil, and pulse to form a chunky puree. Season aggressively with salt and pepper, and set aside.

3. In a sauté pan over medium heat, add the remaining olive oil. Add the tomatoes and the remaining garlic, cooking for 2–3 minutes, until they just start to caramelize, then remove from the heat. Add a full ladle of pesto into the pan.

4. Cook the pasta in the boiling water until just al dente. Drain the pasta, reserving the water. Add the pasta to the pan with the tomatoes and pesto. Add some of the starchy pasta water, and toss to coat. Top with a sprinkle of the Parmigiano-Reggiano, and serve immediately.

Puttin' up pesto

You can refrigerate or freeze the pesto part of this recipe and use it for a quick pasta sauce all on its own.

"**SOME PEOPLE SEE LEFTOVERS AS 'BEEN THERE, DONE THAT,'** but time and time again on *The Chew*, we show that the leftovers from a good meal can be a stepping-stone to a better meal, or one that is just as good. In crafts we don't talk about recycling, we talk about upcycling: taking simple things and using them to make something that looks smart and elegant and is useful. It's the same with food. Look at it this way: if you put a lot of TLC into the food you made last night, or that roast you made during the weekend, you have already created flavor and texture. Now **ALL THAT DELICIOUSNESS** you created the first time is already there, and you just need a little imagination to reinvent it into something that is even more fun because it's front-loaded with flavor. Let the following recipes be a guide to the kind of creative thinking that makes yesterday into a better today. Apologies if that sounds like something that comes out of the mouth of a political candidate, but this is one campaign promise I guarantee, and the proof is on your plate.

Look for this icon (2 FER) for some delicious ways to breathe new life into yesterday's dinner. Once you start making new and **WONDERFUL MEALS OUT OF LEFTOVERS**, you will see that almost any recipe can be the basis for a two-fer, or even a 'three-fer.'"

—Clinton

AT SOME POINT DURING THE WEEK, we'll roast two to four chickens, and then we'll work other dishes off that chicken throughout the week too. Next night we'll do a risotto, or pasta, or maybe we'll repurpose the chicken for tacos, or chili, or that kind of stuff too. Remember, you can toss almost any vegetable, fresh or leftover, into a risotto: radicchio, kale, chard, fennel, etc. Lizzie always makes some kind of chicken salad for a sandwich that you can eat on the fly.

—Michael

INSPIRATION FOR HOW TO USE LEFTOVERS happens to me the way someone else can instantly imagine decorating a room or composing a song. Show me a bag of groceries or a half-full fridge, I can think of thirty meals. I just start thinking that way. I love leftovers, although my kids are a little trickier because they don't want the same dish the next day. So all you've got to do is think that today's steak or pot roast is tomorrow's tacos or enchiladas or ravioli filling. I always think about a transformation that isn't recognizable as yesterday's meal, although still has all that flavor that I spent time putting into it. Anything can become a ragù for pasta; leftover protein or produce chopped up a little bit more and cooked just a little bit, and tossed with good noodles, is delicious. It's a free meal almost.

"**WHAT I LIKE TO START FROM** is a simple preparation, like grilled or roasted meat. My goal is to keep my taste buds excited, so I build a more complex dish the second night that totally changes flavors. For example, if you take a basic tomato soup, the next night you can reduce it down and use it to flavor a different soup or a chili. It's just about seeing the ways that dishes that you plan on making can be versatile in new dishes. Pasta is terrific for leftovers—I never eat a big portion; I like three, four bites and then that's enough for me, because at the end of the day I'm not going to get filled up on pasta in the right way. I need vegetables, I need protein and other stuff in my diet, but I'm also not going to make a quarter cup of pasta. I'll make a decent-sized batch and I'll look for ways to include it and really sauce it up in the days to come."

—Daphne

"**THE BIG IDEA WITH LEFTOVERS** is *cook once and use twice.* While I like leftovers, I don't necessarily need to make my leftovers into something else. I cook with the intention of having that meal again. That doesn't mean it doesn't change. By the second day flavors marry and come together to make new flavors. Now if it's a chicken where I purposefully do two chickens, then I know that chicken's gonna be repurposed for something else, or we'll have a roast and I'll buy a bigger roast than we're going to eat, and it's tomorrow's meatloaf or enchilada or barbecue sandwich. If it was good to begin with, it's going to stay good as long as you are nice to it."

—Carla

Chili Salmon with Mango Cucumber Salsa

SERVES 4 | COOK TIME: 5–7 MINUTES | PREP TIME: 10 MINUTES | COST: $

Easy

The mark of a great salsa is how many things you can serve it with. If that's the way you rate your salsas, this one is near the top. It's great with meats, chips, and fish. I make it for parties and make enough of it to keep in the fridge to liven up leftovers. It starts with the cucumbers, which are great all through summer: cool, refreshing, crunchy, and loaded with filling fiber. Then the centerpiece—fresh mangoes—is great with grilled salmon, skin side down, nice and crispy. One of the cool things we have in New York in June is down on the Lower East Side, where this big tractor trailer full of mangoes arrives and they peel some right there for you, served with some sea salt . . . heaven! And, of course, there's the big daddy of antioxidants: fresh blueberries. Who says healthy food can't be fun food? You won't after you whip up a batch of this fresh salsa.

FOR THE MANGO CUCUMBER SALSA

2 cups mango, peeled and cubed

1 cucumber, peeled and diced

2 avocados, pitted and cubed

½ cup blueberries, rinsed

1 jalapeño, seeded and minced

Zest and juice of 2 limes

½ teaspoon kosher salt

2 tablespoons parsley, chopped

FOR THE SALMON

4 5- to 6-ounce skin-on salmon fillets

3 teaspoons olive oil

2 teaspoons chili powder

Salt

Freshly ground pepper

TO MAKE THE MANGO CUCUMBER SALSA

1. Toss the ingredients in a medium bowl until well mixed. Set aside.

TO MAKE THE SALMON

2. Preheat a grill or grill pan to medium-high. Brush the salmon with olive oil and sprinkle ½ teaspoon chili powder over each of the salmon fillets. Season with salt and pepper, and place, skin side down, onto the grill. Once the skin is crispy, about 2–3 minutes, flip, and continue to cook on other side for an additional 2 minutes, for medium rare, or 3–4 minutes, for medium. Serve alongside the salsa.

Angel Hair with Olive Oil, Garlic, and Chili Flakes

2 FER

SERVES 4 TO 6 | COOK TIME: 5 MINUTES | PREP TIME: 5 MINUTES | COST: $

Easy

Like all chefs, I like a challenge in the kitchen. Regular viewers know that I take pride in doing quick, easy, and cheap meals. This simple dish might take the prize. Three minutes and less than a buck a serving!

Inspiration started with a tweet:

HEY, CHEF SYMON, THE FAMILY IS HUNGRY. PASTA, GARLIC, PARM, BUTTER, CHILI, AND A FULL SPICE CABINET—ANY IDEAS?

Any ideas? That's my middle name! Some spicy heat, some golden pan-roasted garlic, and some fresh parsley finished with Parmesan and butter make for a rich-tasting, super-fast sauce. There are two things to bear in mind: First, you only roast your garlic until it begins to color a little bit—that's the point when it has that great nutty flavor that it loses if you let it cook any longer. Second, the parsley only gets one pass with the knife—any more and you begin to squeeze out the oil, which is where the flavor in parsley lives. With herbs, my motto is "one and done."

If you make too much pasta to eat in one meal, save the noodles and use in the very next recipe.

Salt

1 pound angel hair pasta

4 tablespoons extra virgin olive oil

5 cloves garlic, sliced

1 teaspoon–1 tablespoon chili flakes

1 cup chopped parsley

½ cup freshly grated Parmesan

1 tablespoon butter

1. Bring a large pot of water to a boil and add salt.
2. Add the pasta to the water, occasionally stirring so it doesn't stick together.
3. While the pasta is cooking, heat a 12-inch skillet over low heat. Add the extra virgin olive oil and the garlic, and let cook over low heat for 3 minutes, until the garlic is tender and aromatic. Add the chili flakes.
4. Add 1 cup of the pasta water, and turn the heat up to medium and bring to simmer.
5. Cook the pasta 1 minute less than the package instructions say, then drain the pasta and add to the skillet, stirring to coat the noodles.
6. Remove from the heat. Stir in the parsley, Parmesan, and butter and serve.

Leftover Noodle Pancake with Fall Fruit Slaw

2 FER

SERVES 6 | COOK TIME: 20 MINUTES | PREP TIME: 10 MINUTES | COST: $

Moderate

Like most people, I have those days when I don't feel like shopping or don't have the time, and I also don't feel like making something from scratch. So I open the fridge and see what's there and what the ingredients say to me. It's always something interesting.

One of our viewers, Jamie, sent us a list of the contents of her fridge, and then she asked us to come up with a meal. It was an average American fridge: a few pieces of fruit in the crisper, some soy sauce, half an onion (actually a bunch of halves just waiting to be tossed out because they'd never gotten used), and a bowl of noodles. When I saw those noodles, I knew I had a starting point. I'd make a crispy noodle cake like they do in Chinese restaurants, and then it seemed to me that the apples and nectarines in the fruit drawer could make a nice slaw. It's not a combination I would have come up with all on my own, but they were there and they spoke to me. Moral of the story: listen to your fridge.

FOR THE NOODLE PANCAKE

2 tablespoons extra virgin olive oil

½ onion, sliced

Salt

2 eggs

Pepper

½ pound leftover cooked pasta noodles

2 tablespoons bread crumbs

3 scallions, chopped

1 2-inch ginger, julienned

½ serrano chili, minced

2 tablespoons soy sauce

2 tablespoons rice wine vinegar

TO MAKE THE NOODLE PANCAKE

1. Preheat the oven to 350 °F.

2. In a large ovenproof, nonstick skillet, heat the olive oil to medium heat and add the onion to sauté. Season with salt, and cook until soft, about 4 minutes.

3. Whisk the eggs gently in a large bowl, and season with salt and pepper to taste. Add the pasta to the eggs, along with the sauteed onion and bread crumbs. Add in the rest of the pancake ingredients and toss to coat.

4. Add the contents of the bowl to the large skillet and cook over medium-high heat. Cook until golden and crispy on the bottom, then place in the oven for 10 minutes. Take out of the oven and flip. Place back into the oven for 5 more minutes, until the other side is browned.

FOR THE SPICY FRUIT SLAW

2 nectarines, peaches, or plums, pitted and julienned

2 Granny Smith apples, julienned

½ serrano chili, sliced

2 tablespoons almonds, toasted and chopped

2 jarred cherry peppers, chopped

2 scallions, sliced

2 tablespoons capers

¼ cup basil, chiffonade

Juice of 1 lime

2 tablespoons rice wine vinegar

1 tablespoon soy sauce

Kosher salt

Freshly ground black pepper

TO MAKE THE SPICY FRUIT SLAW

5. Place the thinly sliced nectarines, apples, and serrano chili in a medium bowl. Add the rest of the ingredients and toss with the vinegar and soy. Season with salt and pepper.

6. Plate the noodle pancake on a large platter and top with the spicy fruit slaw.

Grilled Chicken Thighs with Watermelon Feta Salad

2 FER

SERVES 4 WITH LEFTOVERS, OR 8 | COOK TIME: 10 MINUTES

PREP TIME: 5–10 MINUTES | INACTIVE PREP TIME: 2–4 HOURS | COST: $

Easy

I love this easy dish because of its enticing blend of sweet, salty, and savory: watermelon salad with feta—a classic Greek combo. My mom made it for us all the time, and we always ate the whole thing. Also from my Greek heritage: marinating in yogurt, then grilling. We do it with chicken or lamb for a tangy crust. The spices, especially the chipotle, are a bit of a New World mash-up, but the inspiration is Greek. Daphne, who is an endless source of nutritional wisdom, informed us that watermelon is a sexy food because it sends a jolt of blood to—ahem—the right places. I knew there was a reason people love watermelon. If there are any thighs left over—they are the makings of a wonderful Chicken Club (page 47).

FOR THE CHICKEN

8 boneless, skin-on chicken thighs

Kosher salt

1 cup Greek yogurt

Zest and juice of 1 orange

1 tablespoon whole coriander seeds, toasted and ground

2 teaspoons whole cumin seeds, toasted and ground

2 teaspoons chipotle powder

TO MAKE THE CHICKEN

1. Season the thighs liberally with salt. In a gallon-sized zip-top bag, combine the yogurt, orange zest and juice, coriander, cumin, and chipotle. Season with salt. Add the chicken, turn to coat, and refrigerate for 2–4 hours, or put together before work and let marinate until it's time to make dinner!

2. Let the chicken come to room temperature for 30 minutes before grilling.

3. Meanwhile, heat a charcoal or gas grill to medium.

4. Remove the chicken from the bag, wiping off and discarding any excess marinade. Put the chicken on the grill, skin side down, and cover with the lid. Grill for 4–6 minutes, open the lid, and flip the chicken. Put the lid back on, and grill for 5 minutes, until the chicken reaches an internal temp of 160 °F. If using a grill pan, cook the chicken about 5 minutes per side, until cooked in the center. Remove from the grill and let rest while you put the salad together.

FOR THE WATERMELON FETA SALAD

½ small to medium seedless watermelon, cubed

1 cup Greek feta, crumbled

¼ cup mint leaves, torn

3 scallions, sliced

1 clove garlic, grated or finely minced

3 tablespoons red wine vinegar

¼ cup extra virgin olive oil, plus more for garnish

Pepper, to taste

TO MAKE THE WATERMELON FETA SALAD

5. Combine the watermelon, feta, mint, scallions, and garlic in a bowl. Whisk together the red wine vinegar and olive oil. Pour over the salad, season with pepper, and toss to coat.

6. Plate the chicken with a side of watermelon feta salad, and finish with a drizzle of olive oil for garnish.

Grilled Chicken Club

2 FER

SERVES 4 | COOK TIME: 10 MINUTES | PREP TIME: 10 MINUTES | COST: $

Easy

When it comes to chicken leftovers, I'm a thigh man. No insult meant to breasts, which are a fine body part, but the thigh is way more succulent. When we made this on the show, Leo Howard from the Disney show *Kickin' It* was my helper. It turns out this guy is more than a great young martial arts expert and comic actor. He can actually cook! When I asked him how he came to be so comfortable in the kitchen, he came up with one of the best answers: "My parents didn't cook, and I was like, 'Okay, I've got to figure out how to do something to feed myself.'" Molto practical, as we say in Italy.

As for the sandwich, bacon and avocado can make anything taste good, but if you want to go from good to great, make your own condiments instead of reaching for that old jar of ketchup or mayo in the fridge. This lime and jalapeño aioli makes everything taste so fresh and zippy. It's also great with leftover fish.

4 boneless, skin-on chicken thighs

Kosher salt

Freshly cracked black pepper

Olive oil, to brush the grill

8 tablespoons Jalapeño Aioli (recipe follows)

4 kaiser rolls, split and toasted

1 avocado, sliced

10 slices cooked bacon

2 cups arugula

FOR THE JALAPEÑO AIOLI

2 egg yolks

1 jalapeño, seeded, deveined, and minced very finely

Zest and juice of 1 lime

Salt, to taste

Pepper, to taste

1 cup extra virgin olive oil

1. Preheat a grill or grill pan to medium-high heat.

2. Season the chicken thighs with salt and pepper. Brush the grill or grill pan with the olive oil, and place the chicken thighs, skin side down, on the grill. Grill for 4–6 minutes, or until the skin releases easily, and flip and cook another 5 minutes, until the chicken is cooked through.

3. Spread 2 tablespoons of the aioli on the cut side of the top half of the kaiser roll. Stack the chicken, avocado, bacon, and arugula on the bottom half of the roll, and then sandwich with the top.

TO MAKE THE JALAPEÑO AIOLI

4. Place the egg yolks, jalapeño, lime zest, lime juice, salt, and pepper in a large bowl or the bowl of a food processor. Mix just to combine. Slowly add the olive oil until emulsified. Yields ½ cup. This will keep in the fridge for up to a week.

Chicken Marsala

SERVES 4 | COOK TIME: 5 MINUTES | PREP TIME: 10 MINUTES | COST: $

Easy

Since I started doing 5-in-5s on the show (5 ingredients in 5 minutes), viewers have been writing me, asking for tips for quick meals, like this tweet:

YO CHEF SYMON! NEED AN URGENT TIP…I HAVE CHICKEN THIGHS, BUT NOT MUCH TIME OR PATIENCE! HELP!

My answer is the Italian classic Chicken Marsala—only instead of boneless breast, which can get kind of dry, I use boneless thighs because they have nice juicy dark meat. They need to be pounded thin so that they cook quickly. Then when the chicken, mushrooms, and shallots are all cooked, I deglaze the pan with a little Marsala wine and water. You will be surprised how full flavored a sauce can be with just a few ingredients.

4 boneless, skinless chicken thighs, pounded thin

Salt, to taste

Pepper, to taste

Flour, for dredging

5 tablespoons olive oil

2 shallots, thinly sliced

1 pound cremini or white mushrooms, thinly sliced

1 cup Marsala wine

3 tablespoons butter, cubed

⅓ cup parsley, chopped, for garnish

1. Heat a large sauté pan over medium-high heat.
2. Season the chicken thighs with salt and pepper. Dip the chicken in flour on both sides, and shake off the excess flour.
3. Add the olive oil to the hot pan and add the chicken thighs. Cook for 2 minutes on each side, until golden brown and cooked through, and set aside.
4. Add the shallots and mushrooms to the pan. Season with salt and pepper. Cook over medium-high heat, letting the mushrooms brown. Once they have released all their liquid, and it has cooked off, add the Marsala wine. Reduce for a minute, cooking off the wine, then stir in the butter to emulsify. If the sauce is too thick, add a splash of water to loosen.
5. Place the chicken thighs onto a platter and cover with the Marsala mushrooms. Garnish with the chopped parsley.

Chicken Saltimbocca with Capers and Grapefruit

SERVES 6 | COOK TIME: 15 MINUTES | PREP TIME: 20 MINUTES | COST: $

Moderate

I have always loved any recipe with the word *saltimbocca*, which is Italian for "jumps in your mouth." I want something that is so good that it seems to jump onto my fork and then somersaults into my mouth. The traditional saltimbocca is made with veal scallops, prosciutto, and cheese. For my chicken dish, my aim was to pair the food with the wine. Now you know how wine experts are always using phrases like "it has delicious notes of grapefruit" or "it is green and grassy." Instead of taking that as a figure of speech, last night, when I opened a bottle of Pinot Grigio that was described in exactly those terms, I said to myself, "Mario, make something with grapefruit and, for the green part, some green olives." And that's exactly what I did. You can too. Moral of the story: let all that blah blah blah on the wine label give you some ideas on flavors to combine in your next recipe.

1 grapefruit

6 boneless, skin-on chicken thighs, pounded thin

Salt

Pepper

6 tablespoons Parmigiano-Reggiano

6 slices prosciutto

6 toothpicks

All-purpose flour, for dredging

Olive oil, for the pan

2 tablespoons butter

3 cloves garlic, minced

4 tablespoons capers

10 large green olives, cut into quarters

1 cup dry white wine

1. Peel and segment the grapefruit and reserve all the juices. Cut the segments into thirds and set aside.

2. Place a large sauté pan over medium-high heat.

3. Season the chicken thighs with salt and pepper, and place skin side down on a cutting board. Grate Parmigiano-Reggiano evenly on the flesh side of the chicken, and press a piece of prosciutto on top. Fold the thigh in half (so the skin is on the outside), and secure with a toothpick. Dredge in flour and shake off the excess. Repeat with the remaining thighs.

4. Add about 3 tablespoons of olive oil to the pan, and then add the chicken thighs. Work in batches so as not to overcrowd the pan, adding more oil as needed. Brown on each side until golden, 3–4 minutes per side.

5. Drain off the excess oil, leaving about 2 tablespoons in the pan. Add in the butter. Toss in the garlic, capers, and olives. Sauté for 1 minute. Pour in the wine, and bring to a boil. Cook for 30 seconds, and then add

1 cup chicken stock

Juice of 1 lemon

3 tablespoons flat-leaf parsley, chopped

1 endive, sliced ½ inch thick

in the reserved grapefruit juice. Add the chicken stock and swirl to emulsify. Simmer until thick.

6. Take the pan off the heat and adjust the seasoning with the lemon juice, salt, and pepper. Stir in the parsley, endive, and segmented grapefruit. Remove the chicken to a platter along with the sauce.

Drew Barrymore excitedly awaits instructions from Mario.

Hot Sauce Fried Chicken

SERVES 6 TO 8 | **COOK TIME: 12–24 MINUTES** | **PREP TIME: 15 MINUTES**

INACTIVE PREP TIME: UP TO 12 HOURS | **COST: $**

Easy

Some people dream about flying to the moon or winning an Oscar or—even better—winning the lottery! Me? I dream about bacon, as in "How can I include bacon in a dish because I know bacon makes things better?" And then, in a flash of bacon-ized inspiration one night, I thought of one of the all-time crunchiest, crispiest comfort foods—fried chicken. Before I get to the bacon part, I start by marinating my chicken in my favorite hot sauce. Then, when I am ready to rock in front of the skillet, I cook some bacon in my frying oil to add smoky, salty flavor right out of the gate. Just before serving, I top the chicken with more hot sauce, chopped bacon, and scallions. Afterward, I'm ready for a nap and, most likely, another bacon-infused dream.

3 pounds chicken thighs and legs

Kosher salt

Freshly ground black pepper

1 bottle hot sauce

3 cups buttermilk

3 cups flour, for dredging

Vegetable oil, for deep-frying

½ pound bacon

2 scallions, chopped

1. If you have time, start this recipe the night before. Season the chicken pieces generously with salt and pepper. Place the chicken in a resealable bag and pour in the hot sauce. Squeeze out the excess air, and place the bag in a casserole dish (in case the bag leaks). Massage the chicken in the bag, ensuring all the pieces are coated. Marinate in the fridge overnight or as long as you can.

2. Remove the chicken from the marinade and discard the hot sauce. Pour the buttermilk in a shallow container, and place the flour in a shallow container as well. Season the flour with salt and pepper.

3. Set up a resting rack on a sheet tray. Dip the chicken pieces in the buttermilk, and then dredge them in flour and set aside.

4. Preheat a large pot of vegetable oil to 350 °F. Place the bacon in the oil to render. Remove the bacon, once crisp, to a paper towel–lined plate. Once cool, chop.

5. Fry the chicken in batches until golden brown, about 10–12 minutes per batch. Remove the chicken with a slotted spoon to a paper towel–lined plate. Sprinkle with salt immediately. Serve topped with the chopped bacon and scallions.

Dorm Room Chicken Chili

SERVES 4 TO 6 | COOK TIME: 35–40 MINUTES | PREP TIME: 10 MINUTES | COST: $

Easy

Remember those days of microwaved ramen and leftover pizza? I sure do. It's how I put on scads of weight when I started college. As I learned from experience, though, you can eat well, conveniently, and cheaply even on a college student's budget. This chili lops off about 500 calories from traditional chili recipes, but it is still loaded with flavor. Another great thing about it is once you make it, you've got a potful that's good for a few meals throughout the week.

2 tablespoons canola oil
1 large yellow onion, chopped
4 cloves garlic, smashed
4 boneless, skinless chicken breasts, diced
Salt
Pepper
2 medium zucchini, diced
1 8-ounce bag frozen corn, thawed
2 tablespoons tomato paste
1 16-ounce can of roasted tomatoes, chopped
¼ cup chili powder
2–3 tablespoons cumin
2 bay leaves
2 tablespoons oregano
1 chipotle pepper in adobo sauce, chopped
2 15-ounce cans kidney beans, drained and rinsed
1 15-ounce can black beans, drained and rinsed
1 12-ounce bottle beer
1 cup vegetable stock
Shredded Cheddar, to serve
1 avocado, chopped, to serve
Fresh lime juice, to serve
Sour cream, to serve

1. In a large heavy pot, heat the oil over medium-high heat. Add the onion and garlic, and sauté until translucent. Season the chicken with salt and pepper, and add to the pan, cooking for 3 more minutes.

2. Add the zucchini and corn, and sauté for 5 minutes, stirring occasionally. Add the tomato paste and the roasted tomatoes, including the juice. Then add salt, pepper, and all the herbs and spices. Stir well. Add the chipotle pepper and beans.

3. Add the beer and vegetable stock until liquid covers all ingredients in the pot. Bring to a boil, and then reduce heat to medium-low. Simmer for a half hour, stirring occasionally. Remove from the heat, and adjust seasonings to taste.

4. Ladle into bowls and serve with shredded Cheddar, chopped avocado, and fresh lime juice or sour cream.

NOTE: This is great made in a slow cooker too!

60-Second Guacamole

SERVES 4 TO 6 | PREP TIME: 60 SECONDS | COST: $

Easy

On a busy weeknight, if you are looking for something to add some flavor and a little spiciness to fish, poultry, or pork, think guacamole. In Mexico, the birthplace of guacamole, they use cilantro, but I've found that not everyone loves cilantro. *No problema*, I make this one with oregano. The neat thing is that I can make this recipe in 60 seconds. Of course, when I did it on the show, I had help from Mario and Michael. Hey, it still tastes great if you don't happen to have Mario or Michael hanging around your kitchen. If it takes you 120 seconds to make, no big deal. The point is, it's quick, easy, creamy, spicy, and wonderful. Be sure to try with Dorm Room Chicken Chili (page 52).

3 sprigs fresh oregano, chopped

3 ripe avocados, pitted and cubed

3 scallions, thinly sliced

Juice of 2 limes, to taste

Salt, to taste

Freshly ground pepper, to taste

Hot sauce, to taste

1. Place all the ingredients in a bowl, and mash together with a fork or potato masher to the desired texture. Check the seasonings and enjoy. If you are not planning to eat right away, store in an airtight container covered with a piece of plastic wrap rubbed with a little lime juice. This will keep the guacamole from turning brown.

Carla brings Paula Abdul in for a hug.

Grilled Skirt Steak with Cauliflower Hash

2 FER

SERVES 4 TO 6 | COOK TIME: 15–20 MINUTES | PREP TIME: 15 MINUTES | COST: $

Easy

Hash is one of those things everyone likes the minute you say the word. "Hot Salad," which is what hash essentially is, doesn't sound as laid-back and home-cooking-ish as hash. In the wintertime, when fresh vegetables are in short supply, some late-season cauliflower, potatoes, and kale, plus some take-no-prisoners seasoning, fits the bill for comfort food that is nourishing but not super fattening. The full, funky flavor of skirt steak stands up well to the hearty vegetables, but lamb, pork, salmon, or shrimp also fit the bill. It's also good all on its own as a vegetarian meal. If you don't finish all that steak, make yourself a Grilled Skirt Steak Sandwich with Charred Corn Mustard (page 57).

½ pound new potatoes, sliced into ½-inch-thick coins

2 pounds skirt steak

Salt

Freshly ground pepper

¼ cup olive oil, plus more to brush the grill

2 tablespoons butter

½ onion, peeled and diced

½ head cauliflower, cut into florets

1 bunch kale, stemmed and cut into ribbons

2 cloves garlic, sliced

1 teaspoon red chili flakes

1 tablespoon fresh rosemary (leaves only), chopped

2 tablespoons parsley (leaves only), chopped

3 tablespoons red wine vinegar

1. Blanch the potatoes in a pot of boiling salted water for 3–4 minutes. Strain and set aside.

2. Preheat a grill or grill pan to medium-high heat.

3. Season the steak generously with salt and pepper. Brush the grill with olive oil. Grill the steak for 4–5 minutes per side, for medium rare, and set aside to rest.

4. In a large skillet or sauté pan, heat the butter and 2 tablespoons of the extra virgin olive oil over medium-high heat. Add the onion and potatoes in a single even layer. Cook until the potatoes have crisped, and then flip to crisp on other side, about 4 minutes per side.

5. Add the cauliflower and cook, tossing to coat and soften the cauliflower. Add the kale and garlic, and toss so the kale begins to wilt. Add the red chili flakes, rosemary, and parsley. Toss to combine, and finish the dish with the red wine vinegar and a drizzle of olive oil. Transfer to a platter to serve alongside the steak.

Grilled Skirt Steak Sandwich with Charred Corn Mustard

MAKES 4 SANDWICHES | COOK TIME: 10 MINUTES | PREP TIME: 15 MINUTES

COST: $

Moderate

Skirt steak is one of my favorite cuts, both for its deliciousness and the fact that you can serve it well done or medium rare and it is juicy and full flavored either way. Serve on a bun with lettuce and tomato, and you have got a super sandwich. But you know I'm not going to leave it at that. You see, I live in a world where thinking up new condiments is how I keep cooking and, more important, eating more interestingly. Charring the corn develops its inner sweetness and gives a little bit of a bitter edge for contrast. We all like contrast, right, sports fans? And I am a major fan of mustard and vinaigrette. Apparently, so are my cast mates on *The Chew*. Clinton, in particular, took the biggest single bite out of a sandwich that anyone has ever taken in the history of sandwichdom. That's his way of saying *this is the real deal*!

FOR THE SKIRT STEAK

1 pound skirt steak

Salt

Freshly ground pepper

Extra virgin olive oil, to brush the grill

FOR THE CHARRED CORN MUSTARD

1 tablespoon extra virgin olive oil, plus more to brush the grill and for drizzling

2 ears corn, shucked

1 onion, sliced

Salt

Freshly ground pepper

1 tablespoon Dijon mustard

TO MAKE THE SKIRT STEAK

1. Heat a grill or grill pan to medium-high heat.

2. Season the skirt steak generously on both sides with salt and freshly ground pepper. Brush the grill or the grill pan with extra virgin olive oil. Grill the steak for 5 minutes per side, for medium rare. Allow the steak to rest for 10 minutes before slicing.

NOTE: If using leftover steak, just heat through.

TO MAKE THE CHARRED CORN MUSTARD

3. Preheat a grill to medium-high heat. Brush with olive oil. Grill the ears of corn until charred in places, about 5 minutes, rotating throughout the cooking process. Cut the corn off the cob into a bowl.

4. In a sauté pan over low heat, heat 1 tablespoon of olive oil. Add the onion, and season with salt and pepper. Cook about 20 minutes, until the onions are caramelized. Add the caramelized onions to the corn.

1 head romaine lettuce, washed and thinly sliced

2 tablespoons extra virgin olive oil

Zest and juice of 1 lemon

4 kaiser rolls, split, or 1 baguette, sliced

2 beefsteak tomatoes, sliced

5. Add the Dijon mustard to the bowl with the corn and onion, season with salt and freshly ground pepper, and mix well.

TO ASSEMBLE

6. Toss the romaine in 2 tablespoons of the olive oil and the zest and juice of the lemon.

7. Place a few slices of the steak onto each of the kaiser rolls or piece of baguette. Top with some shredded romaine, a big scoop of the corn mustard, and a slice of beefsteak tomato. Season the sandwiches with salt and pepper, and drizzle with extra virgin olive oil.

Slice it the other way

Skirt steak delivers its full juicy flavor when you carve it against the grain.

Pan-Seared Strip Steak with Mushrooms & Caramelized Onions

SERVES 2 TO 4 | COOK TIME: 15–20 MINUTES | PREP TIME: 10 MINUTES | COST: $$

Easy

These ingredients go so well together that you might think that what we have here is a classic recipe. Actually, it came from one of our Fridge Raider segments, where I looked inside an average person's refrigerator and pantry shelves to see how I could make a great piece of steak even greater. The answer? Bacon, beer, onions, garlic, and sour cream, with a little parsley on top. Food scientists will tell you that bacon, steak, and mushrooms are high in that mysterious flavor called umami. If you don't know what that word means, just remember that in the original Japanese, *umami* means "yummy."

2 8-ounce strip steaks

Salt, to taste

Pepper, to taste

3 tablespoons of olive oil, plus more for drizzling

¼ pound bacon, sliced ½ inch thick

1 8-ounce container of button mushrooms, sliced ¼ inch thick

½ onion, thinly sliced

2 cloves garlic, finely minced

½ of 1 12-ounce can of beer

¼ cup sour cream

¼ cup parsley, leaves picked

1. Take the strip steaks out of the fridge 30 minutes prior to use. Season the steaks generously with salt and pepper, and drizzle with olive oil.

2. Heat a medium-sized cast-iron pan over medium-high heat. Put the steaks in the cast-iron pan and cook 3–4 minutes on each side, or until deep golden brown. Take the steaks out of the pan and let rest for at least 10 minutes.

3. In the same pan, add about 3 tablespoons of olive oil and the bacon. Let crisp for 2–3 minutes. Add the mushrooms and toss to coat. Let brown for another 2–3 minutes. Add the onion and garlic, and season everything with salt and pepper. Toss and cook for 1–2 minutes longer, until the onions begin to wilt. Add the beer and bring to a simmer. Reduce by half.

4. Off the heat, add the sour cream and stir to emulsify. Taste and adjust for seasoning. Add the parsley, stir to incorporate.

5. When the steak has rested, slice and plate. Pour the mushroom sauce over the steak and serve.

Fight that flame!

A beautifully cooked steak wants a very hot pan. It also wants some oil to keep it from sticking to the pan. I oil the steak instead of the pan because oil in a pan that hot is a recipe for smoke and fire.

BÜFFET

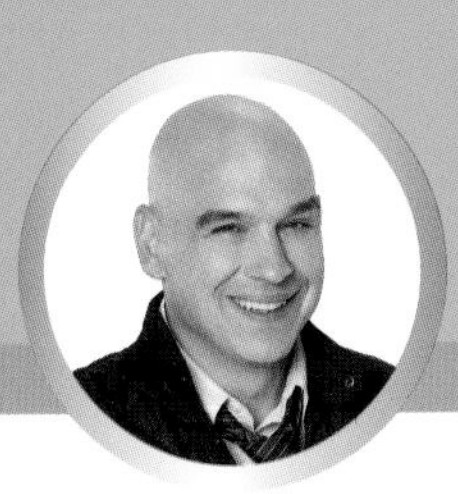

Pork Tenderloin Scallopini

2 FER

SERVES 6 TO 8 | COOK TIME: 5 MINUTES | PREP TIME: 10 MINUTES | COST: $

Easy

A scallopini is a thin, pounded piece of meat, usually from the tenderloin, but it can also be done with chicken breast. The cool thing about it is that you can cook it quickly. This recipe, which I made in 5 minutes on the show, is absolutely crammed with flavor. Crispy, caramelized pork, diced ham, apples, and a rich sauce of apple cider, vinegar, butter, and sage. It's pretty hard to miss with that combo. Don't worry if a little bit of flour sticks to the bottom of the pan; those are the tasty bits that'll make for a super flavorful sauce. And if you don't finish all that pork, put on your Two-Fer thinking cap, turn the page, and use it with Daphne's fried rice.

1–1½ pounds pork tenderloin, cut into 1-inch-thick medallions and pounded thin

Salt, to taste

Pepper, to taste

Flour, for dredging

6 tablespoons olive oil

¼ pound ham steak

3 Granny Smith apples

1 cup apple cider

3 tablespoons butter

2 tablespoons apple cider vinegar

5 sage leaves, plus more for garnish

1. Heat a large sauté pan over medium-high heat.

2. Season the thinly pounded pork with salt and pepper. Dredge in the flour, shaking off any excess. Add 3 tablespoons of the oil to each pan. Carefully lay the pork in the pan and cook for 2 minutes on each side, then remove to a platter and lightly cover to keep warm.

3. Dice the ham into medium-sized pieces. Add the ham to the pan and allow to cook for 1 minute, browning slightly.

4. Dice the apples and add to the ham. Cook for another minute, then add the apple cider. Reduce for 2 minutes, then add the butter. Stir to combine. Finish with the apple cider vinegar and the sage leaves. Adjust seasoning. Nestle the pork back into the sauce to warm through.

5. Plate the pork medallions and top with the sauce. Garnish with sage leaves.

Oz Family Fried Rice

2 FER

SERVES 4 | COOK TIME: 7–10 MINUTES | PREP TIME: 15 MINUTES | COST: $

Easy

Michael's Pork Tenderloin Scallopini is really great, but sometimes even the great Michael's food doesn't get all gobbled up—and you have some leftovers. In the Oz family, leftovers often meant we got to make one of my favorite dishes, Oz Family Fried Rice, which basically is whatever you have in the fridge crisped up with brown rice and amped up with flavor boosters like ginger, garlic, soy, and spicy Sriracha. When my vegetarian mom made it with us on our Mother's Day show, she made it with tofu, but you can do it with pork, chicken, beef . . . whatever. And like my mom said, if you have finicky kids, chances are they're going to like it because it reminds them of fried rice that you get in a Chinese restaurant. There probably isn't a kid on the planet who doesn't love Chinese restaurant fried rice.

3 tablespoons coconut oil

1 onion, diced

½ cup leftover pork, cubed

2 carrots, peeled and diced

6 shiitake mushrooms, stems removed, sliced

1 cup snow peas, stemmed

4 scallions, chopped

2 cloves garlic, minced

2 tablespoons fresh ginger, peeled and grated

2 tablespoons soy sauce

1 tablespoon sesame oil

2 tablespoons rice vinegar

1 teaspoon hot sauce

Kosher salt, to taste

Freshly cracked black pepper, to taste

1 cup cooked rice (I prefer short grain brown rice)

2 eggs, beaten

1 bunch fresh cilantro (leaves only)

1. In a large cast-iron skillet, heat 2 tablespoons coconut oil over high heat. Stir in the onion and cook for 1 minute. Stir in the pork, and cook until golden brown, about 2 minutes.

2. Stir in the carrots, mushrooms, snow peas, scallions, garlic, and ginger, and cook for 2 minutes. In a small bowl, whisk together the soy sauce, sesame oil, rice vinegar, and hot sauce. Add to the pan and stir to coat the vegetables. Season to taste with salt and pepper.

3. Stir in the cooked brown rice and mix thoroughly.

4. In a separate nonstick pan, scramble the eggs in the remaining 1 tablespoon coconut oil and stir into the fried rice, breaking up the eggs as you stir. Adjust the seasoning and serve with the cilantro.

Daphne and Dr. Oz team up to show the *Chew* crew their family favorites.

MEXICAN TORTA | BACON PANCAKES WITH MAPLE BOURBON BUTTER | FRIED CORNISH HENS AND PAN D'ORO FRENCH TOAST | HEIRLOOM TOMATO AND RICOTTA TART

BREAKFAST + DINNER = "BRINNER!"

"**WE ALL KNOW** that when you combine the idea of breakfast and lunch, you get brunch. But many Americans love having breakfast for dinner, or, as we like to call it, "Brinner." It makes so much sense during the work week. Are you too busy to shop? *No problema.* You probably have milk, eggs, cheese, flour, and some veggies in the fridge and on your pantry shelves right now. You say you don't have a lot of time to spend cooking? Well, who does in the morning when you're throwing breakfast together? Breakfasts . . . and Brinners . . . like the **DELICIOUS DISHES** in this section, come together quickly, and they are full of satisfying and fulfilling ingredients to fuel you and ward off the hunger pangs until snack time. And speaking of combining breakfast with other food opportunities, do I hear any votes for **SNACKFAST?**"

—Clinton

Mexican Torta

SERVES 5 | COOK TIME: 5 MINUTES | PREP TIME: 5 MINUTES | COST: $

Easy

Our favorite sandwich here in the USA just might be the good ol' BLT. South of the border, though, you might find the prize taken by the ACE—that's short for avocado, chorizo, and egg. For something so delicious, it's even more satisfying to know you can whip it up in almost no time. On the show—and with Daphne helping—I made it in 3 minutes. And just like the BLT, you can have this for breakfast, lunch, or a quick dinner.

2 tablespoons extra virgin olive oil

1 pound raw chorizo

6 eggs, beaten

Kosher salt

Freshly ground pepper

5 Mexican torta rolls

2 avocados, sliced

1 bunch cilantro, for garnish

1. Heat the olive oil in a skillet over medium-high heat. Add the chorizo and fry, breaking up as it browns. Add the eggs and stir into the sausage. Season generously with salt and pepper. Cook until the eggs form soft curds. Remove from the heat.

2. Split and toast the rolls, and spoon the chorizo-egg mixture onto each of the rolls. Top with slices of avocado, and garnish with the cilantro. Enjoy!

Scramble before you salt

Whenever I make scrambled eggs, I never season them first because the salt will pull water out of the eggs, and who likes watery eggs? Cook your eggs first; salt 'em afterward.

Bacon Pancakes with Maple Bourbon Butter

SERVES 6 | COOK TIME: 13–15 MINUTES | PREP TIME: 15 MINUTES | COST: $

Easy

Kids, young and old, love pancakes, grown-ups love bourbon, and everyone loves maple syrup, so I've put together a heavenly combination of these basic food groups. "Aha," you say, "you've left out one important food group: the bacon group!" Not to worry. I would no more think of skipping the bacon with this than I would make a Margarita without the tequila.

FOR THE PANCAKES

- 8 slices bacon
- 2 cups all-purpose flour
- 2 teaspoons baking powder
- 1 teaspoon baking soda
- ½ teaspoon salt
- 3 tablespoons sugar
- 3 cups buttermilk
- 4 tablespoons melted butter, slightly cooled
- 2 large eggs, lightly beaten

FOR THE SYRUP

- 2 tablespoons bourbon
- 1 cup maple syrup
- 3 tablespoons butter

1. On a griddle over medium-high heat, fry the bacon until crispy, and then transfer to a paper towel–lined plate.

2. Lower the heat to medium, and remove any excess bacon fat. You want there to be a thin layer for the pancakes.

3. Chop the bacon into crumbs, and separate the crumbs into two piles

4. In a medium bowl, combine the flour, baking powder, baking soda, salt, and sugar, whisking together to thoroughly combine.

5. Add the buttermilk, butter, half of the bacon, and eggs, and whisk together until combined but still slightly lumpy.

6. In batches, drop spoonfuls of the batter onto the griddle, and cook until it bubbles, then flip over, about 3 minutes. Transfer to a warm oven while finishing the rest.

TO MAKE THE SYRUP

7. In a small saucepot, combine the bourbon and maple syrup, whisking together over medium heat until thoroughly combined and hot.

8. Cook until reduced slightly, about 5 minutes, then whisk in the butter, a tablespoon at a time, until fully incorporated.

9. Serve a stack of pancakes covered in syrup and sprinkled with the reserved bacon crumbs.

Fried Cornish Hens and Pan d'Oro French Toast

SERVES 6 | COOK TIME: 15–20 MINUTES | PREP TIME: 20 MINUTES

INACTIVE PREP TIME: 12 HOURS | COST: $

Moderate

MARIO: When I see the sign CHICKEN AND WAFFLES on any restaurant, you've got me right there. I usually pull right into the parking lot and order. I am rarely disappointed. I'm going to make mine with French toast—make that Italian toast, using the eggy holiday bread known in Verona as *pan d'oro*, and as *panettone* in Milan. This is a case of less is more, as in don't oversoak; you'll get bread that falls apart. Get it wet, but don't drown it.

MICHAEL: My contribution is spicy, crispy Cornish hen, using half the spices as a dry rub and adding the other half to season up the flour. Cornish hens are great for this because you can serve each person a whole half . . . or should I say half a whole bird? Less carving (and usually cursing) during prep than with a whole bird.

MARIO: And in honor of Daphne's decadent Maple Bourbon Butter, we're going to give the finished product a good dousing.

MICHAEL: My motto is, "Everything is better with bourbon."

FOR THE BUTTERMILK CORNISH HENS

- 2 tablespoons salt
- 1 tablespoon red chili flakes
- 1 tablespoon paprika
- 2 teaspoons cracked black pepper
- 2 teaspoons cayenne pepper
- 2 teaspoons coriander, toasted and crushed
- 2 quarts buttermilk
- 3 Cornish game hens, cut into halves
- Vegetable oil, for deep-frying
- 2 cups flour

TO MAKE THE BUTTERMILK CORNISH HENS

1. In a small bowl, whisk the spices. Pour half into a roasting pan or 2 large Ziploc bags. Pour the buttermilk into the pan or bags. Add the Cornish hens, and move around to coat, making sure the flesh side is submerged in the mixture. Cover and place in the refrigerator overnight to marinate. If you can't find Cornish hens, buy chicken and cut into pieces.

2. Fill a Dutch oven two-thirds of the way full with vegetable oil, preheat to 350 °F.

3. Place the flour in a large baking dish and mix with the reserved spice mixture. Remove the hens from the marinade and discard the liquid. Dredge the hens in the flour mix, making sure to coat heavily.

4. Place the hens in the hot oil 2–3 at a time, depending on space. Overcrowding the pot will prevent

FOR THE PAN D'ORO FRENCH TOAST

5 eggs, beaten

1 cup heavy cream

Zest of 1 orange

1 teaspoon freshly grated nutmeg

1 pinch salt

2 pan d'oro cakes, sliced crosswise into 1½-inch pieces

FOR THE HONEY BOURBON SAUCE

½ cup honey

2 tablespoons bourbon

1 teaspoon paprika

Kosher salt

Freshly cracked black pepper

FOR THE CHIVE AND PARSLEY SALAD

Juice of 1 orange

2 tablespoons olive oil

Salt, to taste

Pepper, to taste

½ cup chives

½ cup parsley

the hens from achieving a crispy crust. Fry for 12–15 minutes, or until you achieve a dark golden crust and the hens are cooked through. Remove and allow to rest on a wire rack. Serve with the warm French toast and honey bourbon sauce.

TO MAKE THE PAN D'ORO FRENCH TOAST

5. Preheat a griddle over medium-high heat.

6. Mix together the eggs, cream, orange zest, nutmeg, and salt in a large baking dish. Place the cake in the mixture, flipping to fully coat.

7. Cook on the griddle for 1–2 minutes, flip, and continue to cook for another 1–2 minutes, or until lightly golden on both sides. Remove from the griddle and continue soaking and cooking the remaining pieces of cake.

TO MAKE THE HONEY BOURBON SAUCE

8. Whisk together all the ingredients, and adjust the seasoning with salt and pepper.

TO MAKE THE CHIVE AND PARSLEY SALAD

9. Whisk together the orange juice and olive oil, and season with salt and pepper. Toss the herbs in the vinaigrette, and then garnish the chicken and French toast with the salad.

Heirloom Tomato and Ricotta Tart

SERVES 6 | COOK TIME: 40–45 MINUTES | PREP TIME: 30 MINUTES

INACTIVE COOK TIME: 30 MINUTES | COST: $

Moderate

When you shop at farmers' markets, my advice is to let the produce speak to you. If it looks good, I buy it, and the recipe sort of builds as I shop. Apart from the fact that things taste better when they are just picked, they also tend to be cheaper. This is one of our favorite quick recipes for when tomatoes are in season. It couldn't be simpler: some dough, tomatoes, basil, ricotta, and seasoning. I like to play with heirloom tomatoes because they all look different, and they're beautiful and delicious.

FOR THE DOUGH
(CAN ALSO USE STORE-BOUGHT)

- 3 cups flour
- Pinch of salt
- 1 tablespoon sugar
- 1½ sticks butter, cold
- ⅓ cup shortening
- 2–4 tablespoons ice water

FOR THE FILLING

- ½ pound heirloom tomatoes, sliced
- ½ bunch thyme, leaves only
- 2 cloves garlic, sliced
- Cracked black pepper
- Salt
- 8 ounces ricotta
- ¼ cup olive oil

TO MAKE THE DOUGH

1. Preheat the oven to 350 °F.
2. Place the flour, salt, and sugar into a food processor, and pulse to combine. Add the cold butter and shortening, and pulse until it resembles coarse crumbs. Add the water until a ball forms. Remove and wrap in plastic. Refrigerate for 30 minutes.
3. Roll out the dough, and press into a tart shell. Dock the dough by pricking all over the bottom. Press in a piece of foil and fill with beans or rice. "Blind" bake for 15 minutes. Remove from oven, discard beans, and let cool.

TO MAKE THE FILLING

4. In a large bowl, combine the tomatoes, thyme, garlic, a few cracks of black pepper, and a large pinch of salt, and toss to coat. Arrange the tomatoes on a baking sheet and roast for 20 minutes. Set aside to cool slightly.
5. Arrange the tomatoes in the blind-baked tart shell. Top with spoonfuls of the ricotta, drizzle with the olive oil, and bake for 15 minutes. Allow to cool slightly before serving.

DORM ROOM APPLE SNACK | POTATO CHIP COOKIES | MICROWAVE CAKE | BANANA ALMOND GELATO | APPLE BROWN BETTY | GRILLED PEACHES WITH ROSEMARY

SWEET TREATS FOR THE MIDDLE OF THE WEEK!

“**WHO DOESN’T LOVE A LITTLE SWEET TREAT?** Either right after dinner or a little bit before bedtime. It puts a little love in your tummy. In my book, nothing beats a homemade dessert. Think about Grandma: She didn’t buy a cake at the store or a premade mix. She got into the kitchen and made it herself. Of course, you may not have the stay-at-home time that lots of grandmas had in the old days, but if you have the basics—**FLOUR, EGGS, BUTTER, SUGAR,** and a little of this and that—you can quickly and easily turn out desserts that beat anything that comes in a box, or a can, or shrink wrap. You can also control the amount of sugar to your taste, rather than the sugar overload in commercial desserts. These desserts will surely send you to bed with **SWEET DREAMS**. And there’s no law that says you can’t make enough dessert to have a few times during the week. In fact, I recommend it.”

—Clinton

Dorm Room Apple Snack

SERVES 4 | **COOK TIME: 5 MINUTES** | **PREP TIME: 5 MINUTES** | **COST: $**

Easy

If necessity is the mother of invention, my dorm room met all the motherhood requirements. There were plenty of healthy food choices, provided they were simple and didn't require a full kitchen. I discovered that there is so much you can do with a blender or, in this case, a microwave. Healthy fruit, nuts, oatmeal, and yogurt combine for a recipe that works as a light meal or a hearty dessert.

- 4 Empire or Granny Smith apples
- 2 tablespoons coconut oil
- 2 tablespoons brown sugar
- 2 tablespoons oats
- 1 tablespoon pecans, chopped
- 1 tablespoon dried cranberries
- 1 teaspoon cinnamon
- ¼ cup apple cider
- 4 tablespoons Greek yogurt
- 2 tablespoons honey

1. Using a melon baller or spoon, scoop out the core of each apple, leaving the bottom intact, to make room for the filling.

2. In a medium bowl, combine the coconut oil, brown sugar, oats, pecans, cranberries, and cinnamon. Stuff the apples with the filling. Place into a microwave-safe bowl and pour the apple cider into the bottom. Microwave on high for 5 minutes.

3. Serve with a dollop of Greek yogurt and drizzled with honey!

Potato Chip Cookies

MAKES 18 COOKIES | COOK TIME: 10–15 MINUTES | PREP TIME:20 MINUTES

COST: $

Easy

If you want to put the black and white cookie on a whole other level, look no further. This dessert is crunchy, crispy, and sweet, which just about covers my basic food groups. I adore it with potato chips, but let your imagination be your guide—if want to try pretzels or tortilla chips, I promise they'll work too. One piece of advice: don't have Michael and Clinton standing alongside you while you mix the batter; they are liable to try to eat it all straight out of the bowl before you even get to make one cookie.

- 1 cup butter, softened
- ¾ cup granulated sugar
- 1¼ cups crushed potato chips
- 1 teaspoon vanilla
- 2 cups all-purpose flour
- Confectioners' sugar, for dusting
- 1 cup chocolate chips

1. Preheat the oven to 350 °F.
2. With a hand mixer, cream the butter and sugar until fluffy. Reduce speed to low and add ¾ cup of the potato chips and mix until incorporated. Add the vanilla and mix until thoroughly combined. Add the flour and mix until just combined—do not overmix the dough!
3. Use a spoon to scoop small 1-inch balls of dough onto a lightly greased sheet pan, spacing them at least 2 inches apart. Dust each of the cookies with a bit of confectioners' sugar, and press flat.
4. Cook for 10–15 minutes, or until golden brown, and cool. Heat the chocolate chips in the microwave or a double boiler until melted, stirring often. Dip each of the cookies in melted chocolate. While the chocolate is still soft, roll the cookies in the remaining crushed potato chips. Allow to set before serving.

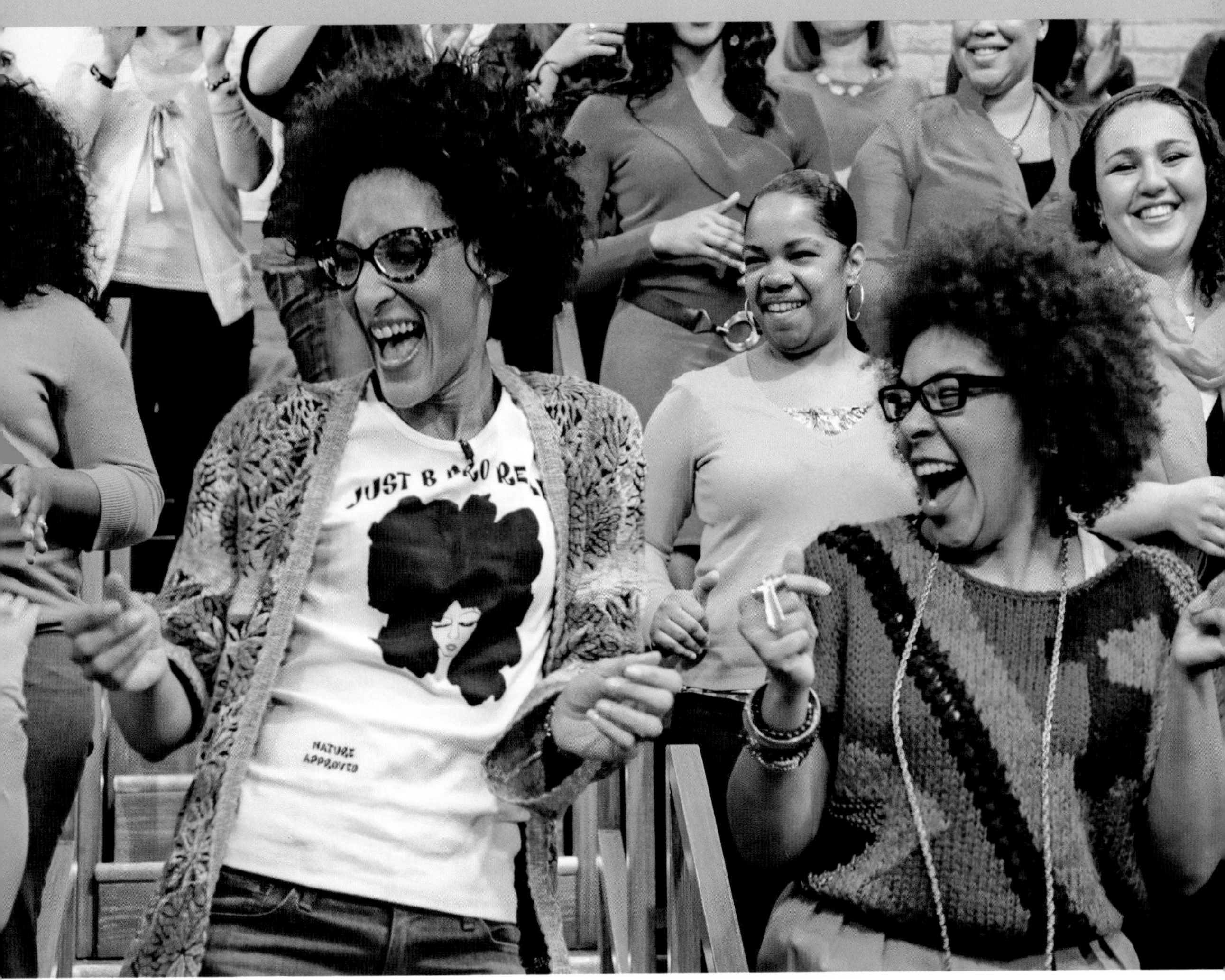

Carla gets her dance on in the audience!

Microwave Cake

SERVES 6 | COOK TIME: 2–4 MINUTES | PREP TIME: 5 MINUTES | COST: $

Easy

I came up with this recipe when I was getting ready for *Chopped All-Stars*, because I knew they'd throw a dessert at me that I'd really have to boogie through in a hurry. Well, how does 3 minutes sound for a gourmet chocolate dessert? Even though it's a pretty casual dessert, remember when you bake that it's important to be precise with your measurements. A roast beef is a lot more forgiving than a birthday cake. Most people think their microwave is just for reheating, but it can be a really good cooking tool, especially when you don't have a lot of extra time on your hands.

FOR THE CAKE

¾ cup flour

¾ cup sugar

Zest of ½ orange

1½ teaspoons salt

4 eggs

2 sticks butter, softened

1⅓ cups chopped dark chocolate

FOR THE WHIPPED CREAM

½ cup heavy cream

¼ cup sugar

Brandied cherries, for garnish

1. In a medium bowl, whisk together the flour, sugar, orange zest, salt, and eggs.

2. Melt the butter and chocolate together in a glass bowl in the microwave.

3. Whisk the melted chocolate mixture into the flour mixture just until combined. Divide the batter among 6 small coffee mugs. Microwave for 1–2 minutes on high and then check it. It should double in size like a soufflé. You may need to add an additional 1–2 minutes to the clock.

4. Meanwhile, whisk the heavy cream until frothy. Add the sugar and continue to whisk until medium stiff peaks form. Garnish the cakes with whipped cream and brandied cherries to serve.

Banana Almond Gelato

SERVES 4 | PREP TIME: 5 MINUTES | COST: $

Easy

4 large bananas

½ cup almond- or hazelnut-flavored liqueur

½ cup almond butter

Pinch of salt

Sliced almonds, for garnish

Amaretti cookies, to serve

1. Put the peeled and sliced bananas in a zip-top bag and place in the freezer until completely frozen.

2. In a blender, add the liqueur, almond butter, bananas, and a generous pinch of salt. Blend until completely smooth, about 2 minutes, or until everything is well combined and has the consistency of gelato.

3. Scoop out into bowls and serve with a sprinkle of almonds and amaretti cookies. Serve immediately.

Apple Brown Betty

SERVES: 8 | COOK TIME: 30 MINUTES | PREP TIME: 10 MINUTES | COST: $

Moderate

What do you make when your guest on *The Chew* is a world-famous race car driver? Pretty simple—you make something quick, which is what we did when Danica Patrick came on the show. Danica is a pretty good cook too, having just made her family's Thanksgiving turkey on the day she visited us. My speedy recipe was one of my family's favorites: Apple Brown Betty. You can make it with yesterday's homemade or store-bought biscuits, if you are the kind of family that ever has any leftover biscuits, or you can use day-old bread or pound cake. The cookie spices give it some flavor high notes, and you can pretty much spice to taste, although I'd say go easy on the cloves because they can take over. "Who was Betty?" you ask. Beats me, but if I ever meet her, I'd give her a big Batali-sized hug.

6 medium Empire or Granny Smith apples

Zest and juice of ½ lemon

4 cups day-old biscuits (recipe follows), bread, or pound cake, cubed

½ cup cold butter

½ cup packed brown sugar

¼ teaspoon ground nutmeg (preferably freshly grated)

¼ teaspoon cloves

Vanilla ice cream, for serving

1. Preheat the oven to 300 °F.

2. Peel and core the apples, and cut them into ¾-inch slices. Transfer to a large bowl. Zest the lemon and squeeze the juice over the apple slices, and toss gently to cover the apples and keep them from browning before baking. Set aside.

3. On a 12-by-17-inch baking sheet, arrange the biscuit (or bread or cake) cubes in one layer and bake on the center rack of the oven until lightly brown, about 10 minutes.

4. Meanwhile, melt the butter in a small saucepan. When the biscuit cubes are done, transfer them to a large bowl, pour half of the melted butter into the bowl, and toss. Set aside.

5. Add the sugar, nutmeg, and cloves to the apples, and gently toss together.

Danica Patrick dives in to the Brown Betty prep work.

6. Raise the oven temperature to 375 °F. Place one-third of the toasted biscuit cubes on the bottom of a 9-inch square baking dish. Top with half the apple slices, followed by another third of the biscuit cubes and then the remaining apples. Top the apples with the remaining biscuit cubes. Pour the remaining butter over everything. Bake on the center rack for 30 minutes, until the top is nicely browned.

7. Remove from the heat and serve warm with vanilla ice cream.

FOR THE BISCUITS

2 cups all-purpose flour

2 teaspoons salt

3 teaspoons baking powder

1 teaspoon baking soda

7 tablespoons cold butter, cut into cubes

1¼ cups Greek yogurt

TO MAKE THE BISCUITS

1. Preheat the oven to 450 °F.

2. Combine the flour, salt, baking powder, and baking soda together in the bowl of a food processor, and pulse until combined. Add the butter, and pulse it a few more times, until the butter is thoroughly cut into the flour mixture.

3. Add the yogurt and pulse the mixture a couple more times to mix it in, just until the mixture forms a cohesive dough. Turn the dough out onto a floured surface and knead just until it comes together. If the dough is too sticky, add a little flour.

4. Press the dough to ¾-inch thickness and cut into rounds using a glass or biscuit cutter, pressing straight down without twisting. Place the biscuits on an ungreased parchment-lined sheet tray. Reshape the remaining dough and cut into biscuits. Bake for 7–9 minutes, or until the biscuits are light golden brown.

Grilled Peaches with Rosemary

SERVES 5 | COOK TIME: 4–6 MINUTES | PREP TIME: 5 MINUTES | COST: $

Easy

I've never met anyone who didn't love grilled peaches. They are sooo good—beautiful, smooth texture and caramelized sweetness. You can do this recipe with many fruits (pineapple or cantaloupe, for example), but peaches get my vote. They go wonderfully with savory herbs, so I like to baste mine with honey and rosemary. You want firm peaches; in other words, they are not super-ripe yet. Save those for eating over the sink when the juice drips down your chin. My fellow Chewsters were totally turned on by this, each of them imagining their own special use for grilled peaches. Mario wanted to make these with grilled chicken. Go for it, Mario. Clinton said they would be nice on a menu with his Ginger Peach Margaritas. I'll drink to that. And Michael, whose thoughts also turn to meat, obsessed about a rib eye with grilled peaches and bleu cheese. I'm down with that too. But for me, they make a simple, yummy weeknight treat.

1 cup lavender honey

1 sprig rosemary

5 peaches, halved and pitted

Olive oil, for drizzling and the grill

1 pint vanilla ice cream, to serve

1. Heat a grill or grill pan over medium-high heat.
2. In a small saucepot, add the honey and rosemary, and simmer for 2–3 minutes over medium heat.
3. Lightly drizzle the peach halves with olive oil. Oil the grill well. Place the peaches cut side down on the grill and cook for 2–3 minutes.
4. Flip the peaches and brush on the warmed honey. Remove once the peaches are warm through.
5. To serve, top with a scoop of ice cream and an extra drizzle of honey.

TGIF

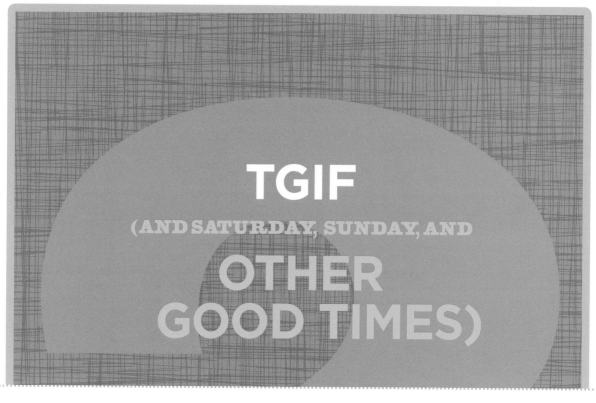

(AND SATURDAY, SUNDAY, AND OTHER GOOD TIMES)

FRIDAY: PIZZA NIGHT, COCKTAIL PARTY

SATURDAY: BIRTHDAY PARTIES,

SATURDAY NIGHT SPECIALS, DATE NIGHT

SUNDAY: SIT-DOWNS

"**WHEN IT'S TIME TO CHILL OUT** or blow it up, *The Chew* is here to help you on special days that put more fun in your food life. We've come up with some **GREAT MEALS** for cocktail parties, birthday parties, brunch, and the anchor of the week in everyone's memory . . . Sunday dinner with the family. Do you want some thoughts about how to put together a birthday menu? We can help you take care of almost everything (except the blowing-out-the-candle part—we think you can handle that without our two cents). Got a hot date? A blind date? Or just a plain good relationship date? Try these recipes and you are sure to get to first base. Need to set your sights on **SOMETHING THAT SATISFIES** your inner chef when you have the time to get down and cook your buns off? Check out our Saturday Night Specials. Cocktail parties can be costly and chaotic, or you can take down the anxiety level and follow some advice from the masters of nibbles, noshes, quenching, and quaffing. These are the recipes that **BRING PEOPLE TOGETHER** when there are no clocks to punch, no tweets to Twitter, no bosses to butter up. You are on your own time. **ENJOY IT!**"

—Clinton

SHANDY | THE C&C PIZZA FACTORY (AKA CLINTON'S AND CARLA'S GRILLED PIZZAS) | TARTE FLAMBÉ | CAKE POPS

PIZZA NIGHT

"**PRETTY MUCH EVERYONE LIKES PIZZA** and pretty much everyone can agree on one thing: they want it *their* way. With sausage or pepperoni? Some onions, olives, mushrooms, or fresh garlic? Red sauce or straight white cheese? One entertaining trick that keeps pizza preferences from escalating into a food fight is to make (or buy) the raw crust and then put toppings out so people can **MIX AND MATCH** to their hearts' content. I'm pretty sure that's how pineapple first wound up in a pizza crust along with some crisp bacon. I laughed when I first heard this un-Italian idea, but guess what? **IT'S DELICIOUS.** The neat thing about putting the toppings out is that when your guests choose their own, they are already halfway to liking it, and I'll take those odds any day. Throwing together a pizza party for a Friday night with the family or a casual game night with friends is **A GREAT WAY TO END THE WEEK** and kick off the weekend."

—Clinton

Shandy

SERVES 2 | PREP TIME: 2 MINUTES | COST: $

Easy

As the grandson of a hop farmer, I was raised on the belief that beer is the great thirst quencher. When I want to "special it up," I make a shandy, which is beer and soda. Of course I prefer Italian soda—in this case, bitter orange soda finished with a splash of Aperol, which is an orange liqueur. You'll be unappetizingly interested to know that its red color comes from a dye made from beetle legs. No lie. I know it sounds weird, but I swear it sure doesn't taste like beetle legs…I think.

1 12-ounce bottle light ale, chilled

1 16-ounce can Italian orange soda, chilled

Splash of Aperol

1. Pour half of the ale and soda into each of the glasses, and top with a splash of Aperol. Serve immediately.

The C&C Pizza Factory
(aka Clinton's and Carla's Grilled Pizzas)

SERVES 4 TO 6 | COOK TIME: 15–20 MINUTES | PREP TIME: 10 MINUTES | COST: $

Easy

CLINTON: These are our favorite pizzas that we make when we're at home. Mine is topped with mozzarella, ricotta, prosciutto, and arugula. I probably make it once a weekend. It's nice hot or at room temperature.

CARLA: Mine is more of a farmers' market topping. That way the vegetables are at their peak flavor and usually their cheapest price, which is a fine combination of virtues. Here we have zucchini, sweet, smoky cherry tomatoes, and crumbled feta, because "feta makes it betta." And different from Clinton's, I'm going to go full-frontal garlic. Love that taste!

Bench flour, for dusting the table

1 ball store-bought pizza dough

½ cup olive oil

FOR CLINTON'S VERSION

2 cloves garlic

1 pound fresh mozzarella ball, sliced

½ cup fresh ricotta

¼ pound prosciutto

2 cups arugula

1. Preheat the oven to 350 °F, and a grill or grill pan to high heat.

2. First cut the pizza dough in half and let it come to room temperature. Using your hands, or a rolling pin, on a floured surface stretch the pizza dough into an oval that will fit on your grill or grill pan, about ¼ inch thick, making sure there is no lip and the dough is evenly flat.

3. Oil your grill or grill pan, and brush the top of your pizza liberally with oil. Place the dough, oiled side down, on the grill or grill pan, and let it cook until it begins to crisp and char, 6–7 minutes. Flip the dough, and begin topping the char side. Reduce the heat to medium-high, or move off the flame, while adding the desired toppings.

TO MAKE CLINTON'S VERSION

1. Rub the crust with the garlic, and then top with the mozzarella and ricotta. Bake for 5 minutes, or until the cheese melts. Remove the pizza from the oven and top with the prosciutto and arugula.

FOR CARLA'S VERSION

½ cup crumbled feta

1 zucchini, sliced into thin coins

1 clove garlic, minced

Zest and juice of 1 lemon

Salt

Pepper

½ cup cherry tomatoes, halved

1 bunch dill

TO MAKE CARLA'S VERSION

1. Sprinkle the crust with the feta, and top with the zucchini, garlic, lemon zest and juice, salt, pepper, and cherry tomatoes. Bake for 5 minutes, or until the cheese melts. Remove the pizza from the oven and top with the fresh dill.

Go easy on the garlic

I like a hint of garlic, but I don't want the flavor of a whole clove. The solution is simple: Smash a clove and rub it over the hot grilled dough just like you would with bruschetta. It will pick up the oils and aroma of fresh garlic but won't overpower you.

Tarte Flambé

SERVES 8 | COOK TIME: 40–45 MINUTES | PREP TIME: 30 MINUTES

INACTIVE PREP TIME: 45 MINUTES | COST: $

Moderate

This cheesy onion pizza is something that French bakers used to make to check the heat of their wood-burning ovens. If the dough caught on fire (flambé), the oven was too hot. Pretty clever, those French bakers. Even cleverer: this Italian American flambés his with some grappa or kirsch. I caution you, these get gobbled up quickly. Make enough.

FOR THE PIZZA DOUGH

- ¼ cup white wine
- ¾ cup warm water
- 1½ ounces yeast
- 1 tablespoon honey
- 1 teaspoon kosher salt
- 1 tablespoon extra virgin olive oil
- 3 cups all-purpose flour, plus more for dusting

FOR THE TOPPING

- Salt
- 2 russet potatoes, peeled
- ½ pound slab bacon, cut into lardons
- 1 tablespoon olive oil
- 1 large Spanish onion, thinly sliced
- 3 cloves garlic, minced
- 4 ounces grappa (Italian brandy) or kirsch
- ½ cup crème fraîche
- ⅓ cup Emmentaler (Swiss cheese)

TO MAKE THE PIZZA DOUGH

1. Combine the wine, water, and yeast in a large bowl, and stir until dissolved. Add the honey, salt, and olive oil, and mix thoroughly. Start by adding 1 cup of the flour and make a wet paste. Add the remaining flour and incorporate.

2. Place the dough on a lightly floured board and knead for 2–3 minutes.

3. Place the dough in a lightly oiled bowl and cover with a towel. Let rise for 45 minutes.

TO MAKE THE TOPPING

4. Preheat the oven to 400 °F.

5. Bring a pot of water to a boil and season generously with salt. Cook the potatoes until they can be pierced easily with a knife, about 20–25 minutes. Remove from the water and let cool.

6. Place the bacon in a large cast-iron skillet. Add the olive oil so the bacon doesn't stick. Cook over medium-low heat until crisp and brown. Remove the bacon from the pan and set aside on paper towels.

7. Add the onions to the pan, and season with salt. Cook until golden brown. Add the minced garlic. Remove the pan from the heat and pour in the kirsch

⅓ cup ricotta

Freshly cracked black pepper

¼ cup chives, chopped

or grappa, and add the flame to the alcohol (carefully!). Return the pan to the heat and cook off the liquid. Let the onions take on color, cooking about 10 more minutes. Once the onions are caramelized, set them aside.

8. Cut the potatoes in ⅛-inch slices. Combine the crème fraîche, Emmentaler, and ricotta. Add about 20 turns of cracked black pepper and ½ teaspoon of salt.

9. Roll the dough out to the size of a cookie sheet or a half sheet pan. Lay the dough onto the pan and cook in the oven for about 4 minutes.

10. Remove the dough from the oven. Smear the dough with the cheese mixture, and shingle the potatoes in a pinwheel pattern. Then place an even layer of the caramelized onions on the potatoes and sprinkle the bacon on top of the onions. Top with a bit more grated Emmentaler.

11. Return the dough to the oven until the dough is crisp on the bottom and the toppings are bubbly, 6–8 minutes. Sprinkle with the chives and serve.

Cake Pops

SERVES 20 TO 24 | COOK TIME: 10–15 MINUTES | PREP TIME: 1 HOUR

INACTIVE PREP TIME: 30 MINUTES | COST: $

Moderate

If you are a cake baker/maker, then you know how you get all that leftover cake when you trim the baked layers of a circular cake. Don't throw it out! What you have is the makings of a great fork-free dessert. Break up the cake, mix it with some frosting or peanut butter or anything sweet and creamy to bind it, then shape it in a little ball, roll it in some crushed nuts or coconut or chocolate bits, put it on a stick, and you have some fine individual desserts that taste supremo but don't get your hands one bit dirty.

FOR THE BASE

1 recipe boxed white cake (your favorite recipe)

1½ cups butter (room temperature)

4½ cups powdered sugar

1 tablespoon vanilla extract

2 tablespoons milk

FOR THE PEANUT BUTTER CAKE POPS

¼ cup peanut butter

2 heaping teaspoons grape jelly

1 cup dark chocolate, melted

½ cup peanuts, chopped

FOR THE COCONUT CAKE POPS

½ cup desiccated coconut, plus more to roll through

½ teaspoon coconut extract

1 tablespoon coconut milk

1 cup dark chocolate, melted

TO MAKE THE BASE

1. Make the cake according to package instructions, allow it to cool, and then crumble. The cake should be crumbs. Split into 2 batches of 5 cups of crumbs.

2. Next make the buttercream frosting. Whip the butter and powdered sugar in an electric mixer on low. Once incorporated, add the vanilla and increase speed to high, mixing until fluffy. Add 1 tablespoon of milk at a time until you've reached your desired consistency. Should yield about 3 cups of buttercream. Split the buttercream into 2 batches.

TO MAKE THE PEANUT BUTTER CAKE POPS

3. Fold the peanut butter into one of the batches of buttercream frosting and set aside.

4. Combine the peanut butter frosting and jelly, and mix into one of the batches of cake crumbs. Roll the mixture into golf ball–sized balls. Insert a Popsicle stick into each ball, and place on a parchment-lined sheet pan. Repeat until all of the mixture has been used up, and then place in the freezer to set for 30 minutes.

5. Once they have chilled, dip the pops into the melted chocolate, and then roll the chocolate-dipped pops

through the peanuts. Return to the parchment-lined sheet pan and return to the freezer until all pops have set.

TO MAKE THE COCONUT CAKE POPS

6. Stir the remaining buttercream, coconut, coconut extract, and coconut milk into the second batch of cake crumbs until it forms a uniform consistency. Form into golf ball–sized balls. Insert a Popsicle stick into each of them, and then arrange on a parchment-lined sheet pan. Repeat until all of the mixture has been used up, and then place in the freezer to set for 30 minutes.

7. Once they have chilled, dip the pops into the melted chocolate, and then roll the chocolate-dipped pops through the coconut. Return to the parchment-lined sheet pan and return to the freezer until all the pops are set.

8. Remove the pops from the freezer when set and allow to come to room temperature before serving.

PERFECT MANHATTAN | EGGNOG | CHEESE CRISPS | PUMPKIN FRITTERS | CLINTON'S CRAFT CORNER: DON'T THROW OUT THE TAKEOUT | HANKY PANKY | SPICY LAMB MEATBALLS WITH CUCUMBER DIP | ROSEMARY SHRIMP WITH ALMONDS | BAKED BRIE BITES | BUTTERSCOTCH TRUFFLES

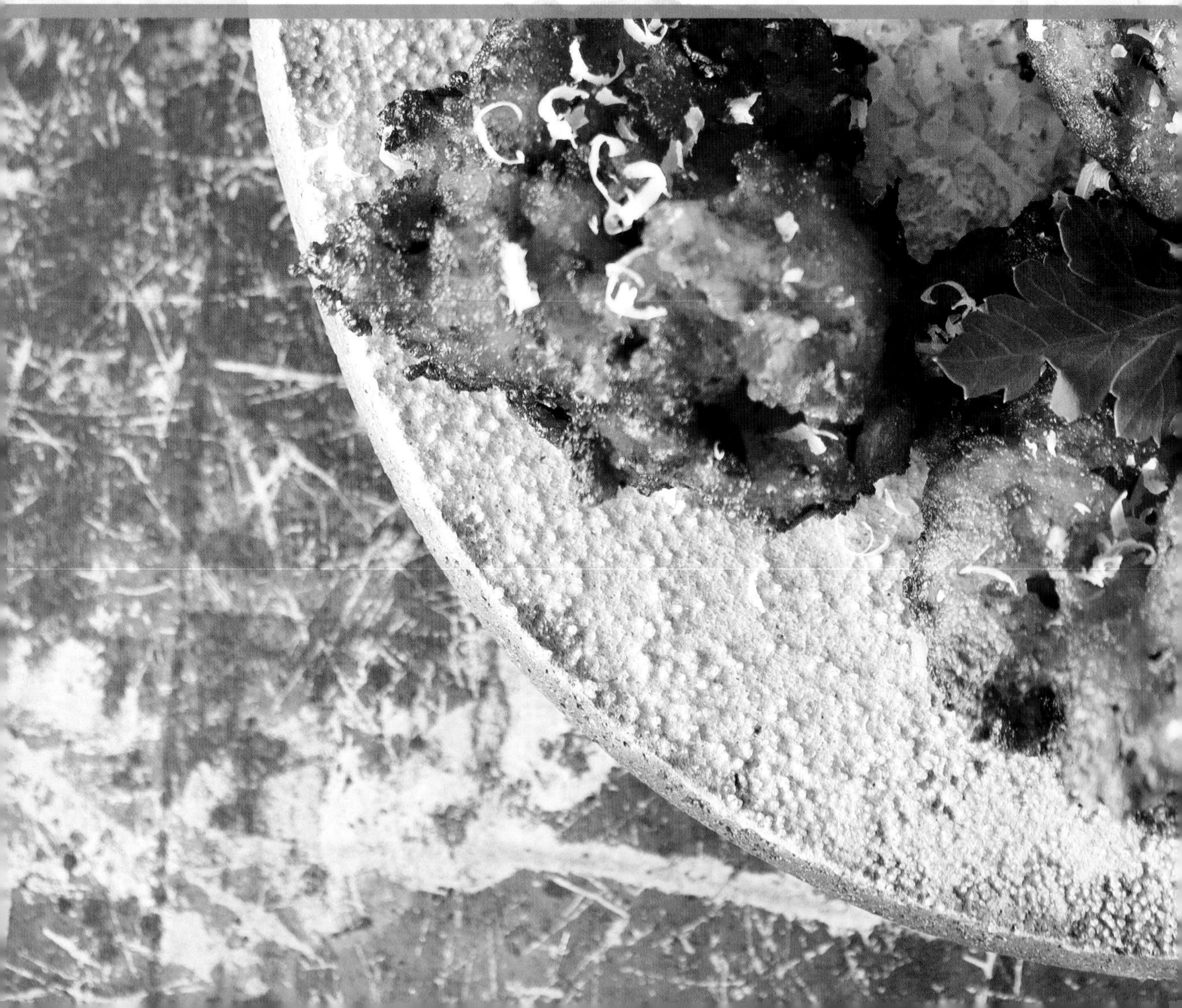

FRIDAY NIGHT COCKTAIL PARTY

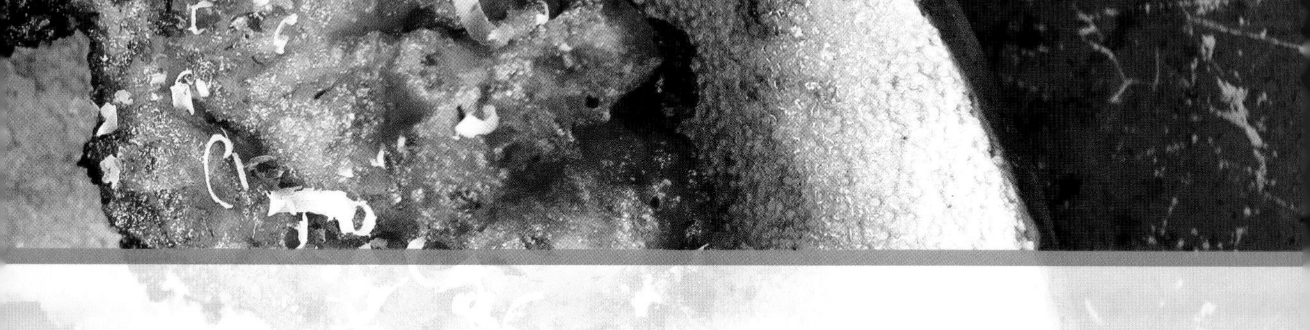

"COCKTAILS AND CONVERSATION go hand in hand. There's nothing like having a glass of wine or having a drink and chatting with someone until the wee hours of the night. I love a cocktail party more than anything, and I also love socializing with friends.

I put a lot of thought into my cocktail parties. I think, "Where am I going to place the food? Where am I going to place the drinks?" I would never put the food in the way of the drinks. You need to separate the two so that people have some mingling room in between, because that's generally where most of the conversation takes place at a cocktail party—in between the food and the drinks.

I love that at cocktail parties you are usually standing up so **IT'S EASY TO MINGLE.** There's a real art form to navigating through a cocktail party. How do you extricate yourself from a conversation that you just think is the most boring conversation in the world? Or how do you find your way to talk to somebody on the other side of the room? I see it as a game or a challenge.

So what makes for a great cocktail party? I asked the crew."

—Clinton

"FIRST, I THINK OF THE PRACTICALITIES. Where are you going to have it? I mean, I think the best room for a cocktail party is the kitchen, because you can always set up a little bar somewhere in the kitchen. I like being able to be by the stove so I can continue to make things while everyone is talking and kinda pass food around and talk.

Next—and I think this is the biggest question—what are you going to serve and how much? Often, the biggest mistake at a cocktail party is portions that are too big and unwieldy. Take sandwiches for instance: it's awkward, trying to hold your drink, hold your sandwich, eat it, use your napkin, talk. You need five arms. Someone is going to make a mess at some point. Instead, I like doing kebabs or any kind of food on a stick. Whatever you do, it should be one or two bites. Even sliders to me don't make any sense because it's not like you can eat a slider in a bite, it's a four-bite thing—one of the big mistakes is serving a meal instead of a bite. Baby lamb racks are two bites. If you did little lamb sausages, and put them on an end of a kebab and grilled them, that's a bite or two. If you do tempura shrimp and passed them around, that's a bite or two. My extra-special signature treat is for specialty things that I always do. For example, I do little lamb chops with lavender salt. So different, so delicious. The main thing is, think bites and go from there."

"AS MUCH AS I LOVE GOING TO A PARTY that has really delicious passed hors d'oeuvres, I don't have the patience to make them, nor do I like them when I do. So I try to make things that you can serve yourself on small plates. It's a little less portion controlled than grabby passed hors d'oeuvres, but it means a lot less time in your preparation. I'll often make marinated olives, a cool cooked or lightly pickled vegetable salad in the way that the Italians do it, or a room temperature fritto misto. I love (make that LOVE!) a tortilla Española or a quiche, cut into little cubes. I'll always have some nice cured meats and cheeses and make those a centerpiece with different condiments. Wine for sure, beer too."

"**A LOT OF OUR HOME ENTERTAINING** is more on the order of a cocktail party because we live in an apartment in New York City, so there's not always seating space for everyone we want to have over. Serving things on scoop chips is an ideal solution, like in my fish taco specialty: I take a little piece of fish, guacamole, and cabbage slaw and put them on a bite-sized chip.

I also like to mix sweet and savory right from the start. The dieting plus here is that when I eat sweet in the beginning of my meal, I'm less tempted to eat dessert, and when you are deep in conversation at a cocktail party, you can scarf up the brownies and the petits fours without even thinking. One of my fave sweet and savory things is a broiled date stuffed with goat cheese and pecans. I'm sure Michael would wrap it in bacon too, which is not a bad idea now that I mention it.

One house rule is you have to serve wine and juices too (that's for you, Carla!). Not everyone likes cocktails. I'd have one white wine, one red, one sparkling.

For cocktails, if I'm doing a themed party, I'll pick a favorite cocktail, like my "sombrero aloha," which is kava or tequila, lime juice, pineapple juice, and a splash of soda water. I would do the pineapple and lime juice together in a little pitcher, and then set the tequila and soda out so people can mix their own drinks."

I HAVE SOME PRETTY SIMPLE RULES. You have to serve about seven things. People feel like they have choices then.

1. You have something on a stick, such as chicken satay or vodka shrimp (if you put shrimp on a buffet, some shrimpaholic is going to eat 'em all).

2. Something that's not on a stick, like little grilled cheese sandwiches.

3. Something that's gooey or liquid, or soups in a demitasse (espresso cup).

4. Something that's stationary, where you serve yourself, say, a macaroni and cheese bundle, or coq au vin with the chicken deboned and in smaller pieces.

5. Something that's passed, like spanakopita. Whatever it is, keep those babies moving.

6. Meat: maybe mini beef Wellingtons. Passed or assemble your own. Instead of wrapping in pastry, you set out pastry pieces, mushrooms, gravy, etc., and guests can assemble their own. The nine-dollar word for this would be *deconstructed*.

7. Roasted vegetables in bowls nestled on a big platter so it doesn't look messy as people dig in. You can keep refilling the bowls as needed.

For dessert, although a big honkin' piece of cake looks beautiful on display, when you start to cut pieces from it, the looks kind of go downhill. I stick with smaller desserts, like tartlets in mini muffin tins, or fruit turnovers instead of big pies. A chocolate fountain with things like fresh fruit, marshmallows, and Rice Krispies Treats for dipping always scores big.

—Carla

Perfect Manhattan

SERVES 1 | **PREP TIME: 5 MINUTES** | **COST: $**

Easy

The first time somebody asked me if I wanted a perfect Manhattan, I answered, "Of course." I mean, who doesn't want *perfect*? Little did I know that the word *perfect* means that you use equal parts of sweet and dry vermouth. The classic calls for rye, but the bourbon Manhattan has made a run at the Manhattan mixologist's manual. My advice is try 'em both and decide. There ain't no bad option.

Ice

2 ounces rye whiskey

¾ ounce sweet vermouth

¾ ounce dry vermouth

4 dashes angostura bitters

1 brandy-soaked or high-end Maraschino cherry, to garnish

1. Chill a martini glass in the freezer.
2. Fill a cocktail shaker with ice. Add the rye, vermouths, and bitters. Stir vigorously for 15–30 seconds.
3. Strain the liquid into the chilled glass and garnish with the cherry.

Lara Spencer shakin' it with Carla during a commercial break.

Eggnog

SERVES 8 TO 10 | PREP TIME: 10 MINUTES | COST: $

Moderate

Eggnog is a classic holiday party drink. I mean, you never see someone walk into a bar and say, "Gimme an eggnog…shaken, not stirred." But it's so good it seems a shame to have it once or twice and then have to wait a whole year. For my version, I threw a party for my liquor cabinet; in addition to the traditional rum, I toss in some bourbon and brandy for good measure. Guaranteed to bring you glad tidings and good cheer even when it's not Christmastime.

8 pasteurized eggs, separated
⅓ cup sugar
1 teaspoon salt
1 cup bourbon
1 cup rum
½ cup brandy
1 quart half-and-half
2 cups whipping cream
Freshly grated nutmeg

1. Beat the egg yolks, sugar, and salt until thick and lemon colored. Gradually add the bourbon, rum, and brandy, beating constantly.

2. Combine the half-and-half and whipping cream, and beat into the egg yolk mixture.

3. Whip the egg whites until soft peaks form. Gently fold into the egg yolk mixture. Stir in salt and chill thoroughly. Grate fresh nutmeg on top before serving.

Cheese Crisps

SERVES 8 TO 10 | COOK TIME: 5–8 MINUTES | PREP TIME: 5 MINUTES | COST: $

Easy

Last thing you want when you're getting reading for a cocktail party is to slave for hours and hours. As they say where I come from: "Ain't nobody got time for that." Well, I'm here to tell you that these scrumptious cheese crisps can be made super quick. Some herbs, some spices, a slice of cheese, and a few minutes in the oven. What could be simpler? They come out lacy and crisp. It works with most hard cheeses. For Cheddar, it works best with aged Cheddar; fresher Cheddars come out a little soft and oily.

1 10-ounce block Gruyère (or other hard cheese)

Caraway seeds

Black pepper

Almonds, chopped

Sesame seeds

1. Preheat the oven to 350 °F.
2. Shave long strips of cheese with a peeler, approximately 1½ inches by 3 inches.
3. Lay the cheese on a baking sheet lined with a silicone nonstick baking mat. Sprinkle with your choice of caraway seeds, black pepper, almonds, or sesame seeds. Or combine the ingredients to make your own unique cheese stick creations.
4. Bake for about 5–8 minutes, or until the cheese is melted, bubbly and golden brown. Remove from the oven and let the cheese sticks cool until ready to handle.

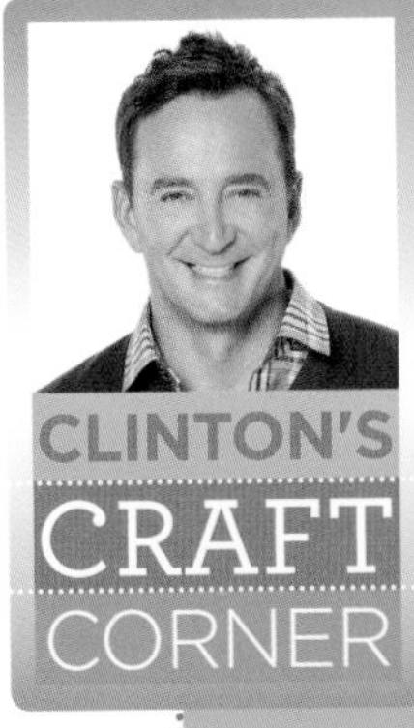

Tip:

"Hey, Clinton," one of our viewers asked in a video she sent in, "after I spend all that money on food and drinks, there isn't a lot left over for decor. Help!"

Home decor help is my middle name. This super-inexpensive tabletop tip also takes the guesswork out of which cheese is which and what's inside those stuffed hors d'oeuvres. This spells it out for your guests.

Place your cheeses and other hors d'oeuvre selections directly onto butcher paper. Then you can simply write on the paper to identify the food. Butcher paper can also be used for a tablecloth, writing your guests' names rather than using place cards or providing a kids' table with crayons to keep the younger guests occupied.

Pumpkin Fritters

SERVES 6 TO 8 | COOK TIME: 5 MINUTES | PREP TIME: 5 MINUTES | COST: $

Easy to Moderate

Sweet, savory, cheesy. What could be better than that except for having a tall supermodel like Carla Hall standing next to you when you make it? All I can give you is the recipe. You'll have to ask Carla to join you on your own. Because these fritters are fried and crispy, they are big favorites with kids, so it's a great way to get them to scarf down their vegetables. By the way, if you don't have pumpkins around, squash will do, even cabbage. You heard me: even cabbage tastes exciting in this recipe.

1½ cups fresh or canned pumpkin puree or butternut squash puree (see Note)

2 large eggs

½ cup unbleached all-purpose flour

½ teaspoon baking powder

1 teaspoon kosher salt

¾ cup grated Parmigiano-Reggiano, plus more for garnish

¼ cup fresh flat-leaf parsley, finely chopped, plus more for garnish

⅛ teaspoon freshly grated nutmeg

Finely ground black pepper, to taste

Olive oil, for deep-frying

Good balsamic vinegar, for garnish

1. Place the pumpkin puree in a medium bowl. Lightly beat the eggs with a fork and stir them into the pumpkin with a wooden spoon or spatula. In another bowl, whisk together the flour, baking powder, and salt. Add the dry ingredients to the puree mixture, along with the grated cheese, parsley, nutmeg, and a pinch of black pepper. Use the wooden spoon or fork to combine all the ingredients into a light batter; be careful not to overmix it.

2. Heat the olive oil to 360°F in a heavy-bottomed pot. Fill the pot no more than two-thirds of the way full, allowing room for the oil to expand. Drop heaping tablespoons of the batter into the oil, and cook until the fritters are golden brown. Fry in batches, cooking for about 2 minutes per side.

3. Drain the fritters on paper towels and season with salt. Garnish with Parmigiano, parsley, and balsamic vinegar.

NOTE: If you are using a fresh pumpkin, cut the pumpkin and scrape out the seeds and stringy bits. Rub the inside with olive oil (or softened butter), and season with salt. Place the cut side down on a sheet tray lined with parchment and cook in the oven at 400 °F until soft, about 40–45 minutes. Scrape out the puree and toss the skins.

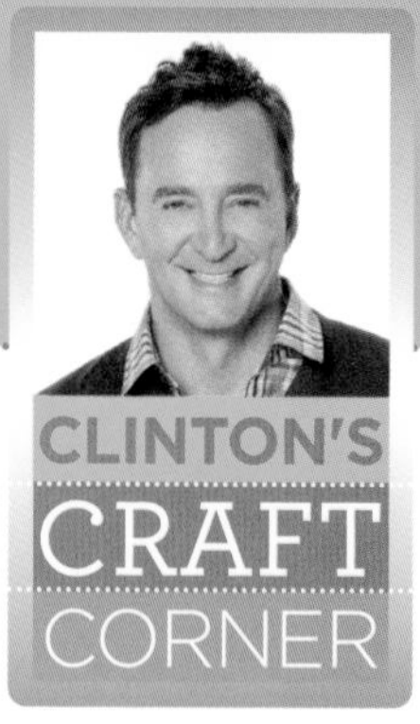

Don't throw out the takeout

Bet you didn't know there was something you could do with used take-out containers from the Chinese place, apart from recycling or tossing in the fire. In fact, you can use them to make really neat decorative hanging lanterns for your cocktail party.

WHAT YOU NEED

Chinese food take-out containers

Pencil

Ruler

Hole punch

Paint

Brushes

Sponges

Twine or ribbon

Tea lights

HOW TO MAKE IT

1. Remove the metal handles from the containers and unfold them to lie flat.
2. Sketch the desired designs with a pencil, using a ruler to help with straight lines.
3. Using a hole punch, punch out circles along the lines of your design. Be sure to also punch out the holes from the handles so that you will be able to put string through them later.
4. If you would like to change the color of your containers, paint them in any color with a brush, using sponges to add texture. Set them aside to dry.
5. Reassemble the containers, stringing twine or ribbon through the holes where the handles once were. Put a tea light candle inside the container and hang for your celebration!

Hanky Panky

SERVES 10 | COOK TIME: 12–15 MINUTES | PREP TIME: 5 MINUTES | COST: $

Easy

A midwestern Cleveland classic. There's almost no party in my hometown that doesn't start with this. It's our version of a bruschetta—a little something on toast. The "classic" is made with sausage and Velveeta. No prob—it's delicious—but my chef's version has Parmesan because, well, that's the cheese I like. I asked my parents when I was a little boy why it's called a Hanky Panky, and they said, "Ask us when you're grown up." I never did find out why, but I now know what Hanky Panky means, and I approve.

1 pound spicy Italian sausage, casing removed

2 tablespoons flour

2 cups milk

½ cup grated Parmesan

½ cup parsley, chopped, plus more for garnish

Salt

Pepper

1 baguette, sliced into 1-inch rounds

1. Preheat the broiler to high.

2. In a large skillet, sauté the sausage until cooked through, about 5–10 minutes. Be sure to break up any large chunks. When cooked, drain, reserving 2 tablespoons of the fat. Set the sausage aside.

3. Whisk the flour into the reserved fat and cook for 2 minutes. Then add the milk. Cook until the mixture thickens slightly, then add the grated Parmesan, parsley, cooked sausage, salt, and pepper. Mix to combine.

4. Heat a grill or grill pan over medium heat. Grill the slices of baguette, transfer to a sheet tray, and spoon the sausage mixture on top. Place in the oven under the broiler until golden and bubbling, about 2 minutes. Remove from the oven and garnish with chopped parsley.

Spicy Lamb Meatballs with Cucumber Dip

SERVES 8 TO 10 | COOK TIME: 15–20 MINUTES | PREP TIME: 15 MINUTES | INACTIVE COOK TIME: 20–30 MINUTES | COST: $

Easy

When you think of meatballs, most folks don't think of lamb first. But it's such a good, economical meat, we ought to. My Turkish ancestors sure loved it. Michael's Greek grandparents too. It accepts aromatic spices really well and a little bit of fiery heat. Instead of pan roasting and braising, which is the classic way to go, mine are baked in the oven, which makes for a lot less fuss. And alongside them I serve a cooling yogurt dip inspired by Indian raita. It tames that first spicy kick you get from the lamb.

FOR THE MEATBALLS

2 tablespoons butter

1¼ cups white onions, finely chopped

1 tablespoon garlic, finely minced

1 jalapeño, finely chopped

1 teaspoon curry powder

1½ teaspoons ground cumin

1 teaspoon ground coriander

½ teaspoon turmeric

Salt, to taste

Freshly cracked black pepper, to taste

1½ pounds lean ground lamb

½ cup fresh whole wheat bread crumbs

⅓ cup fresh parsley, chopped

1 egg, beaten

Zest and juice of 1 orange

TO MAKE THE MEATBALLS

1. Preheat the oven to 375 °F.

2. Heat a large sauté pan over medium-high heat and add the butter. Stir in the onions and cook for 1–2 minutes, and then add the garlic and jalapeño. Cook for another 2–3 minutes, or until the onion turns soft and translucent.

3. Stir in the curry powder, cumin, coriander, and turmeric. Season with salt and pepper. Cook for another minute, or until the onion mixture is fragrant. Take off the heat and let the mixture cool to room temperature.

4. Put the lamb in a large mixing bowl and add the cooled onion mixture, bread crumbs, parsley, and egg. Add in 2 teaspoons of the orange zest and squeeze in about 1 tablespoon of the orange juice. Season with salt and pepper. Mix thoroughly and then form the mixture into meatballs, each a little smaller than a golf ball. Place onto a parchment-lined baking sheet.

5. Put the meatballs in the oven for 15–20 minutes, or until deep golden brown. When the meatballs are done, remove from the oven and let rest. Place the meatballs onto a platter and serve with the raita.

FOR THE RAITA

½ cup English cucumber, peeled, seeded, and diced small

Salt, to taste

1 cup Greek yogurt

2 tablespoons fresh mint, chopped

1½ teaspoons ground cumin

Pepper, to taste

TO MAKE THE RAITA

6. Sprinkle the cucumbers with an even coat of salt and transfer to a sieve. Let drain.

7. After 20–30 minutes, press the cucumbers with a spoon to release any excess water, and then stir them into the yogurt, along with the mint. Add the cumin to the yogurt, and season with salt and pepper. Chill before serving.

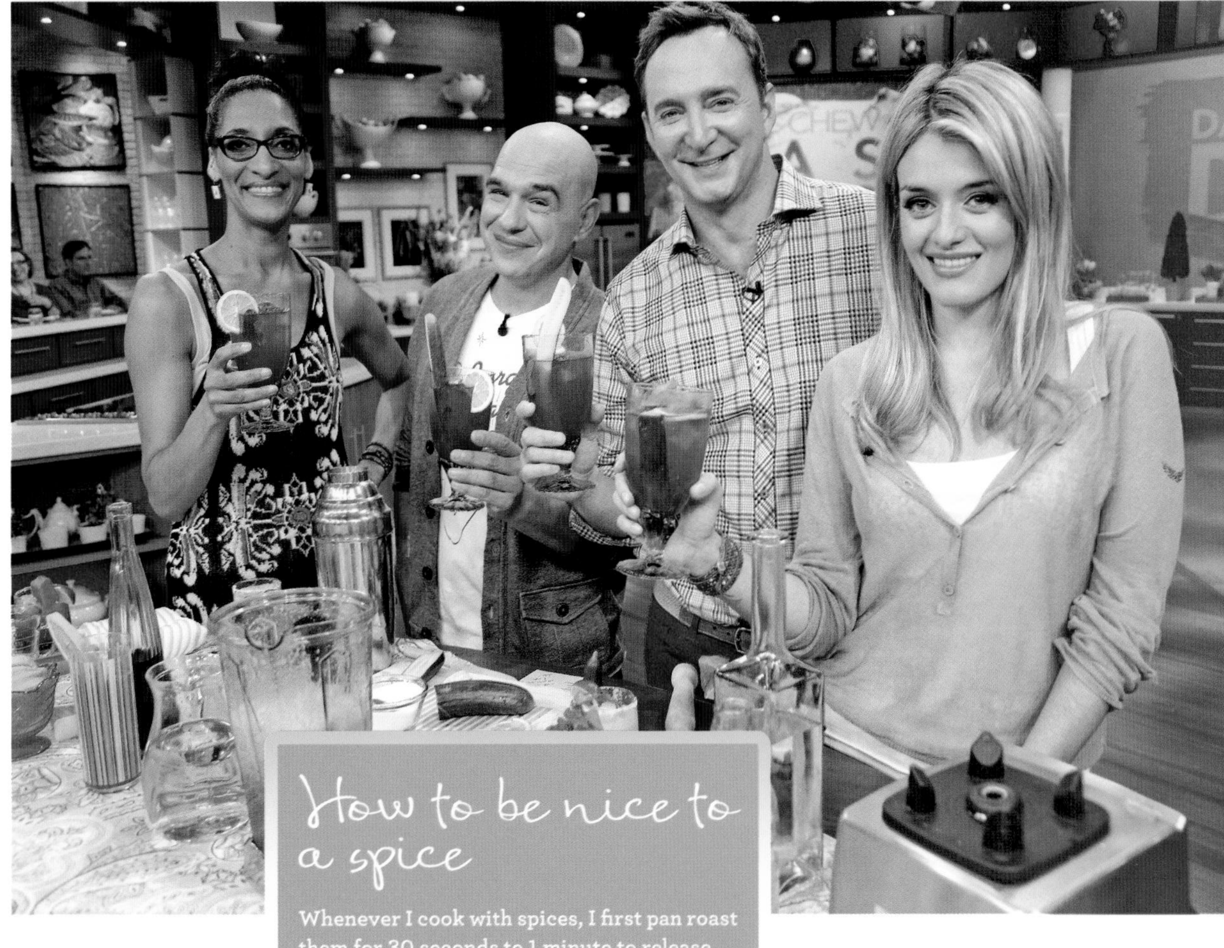

How to be nice to a spice

Whenever I cook with spices, I first pan roast them for 30 seconds to 1 minute to release their oils. That's where all the flavor is.

Rosemary Shrimp with Almonds

SERVES 8 TO 10 | COOK TIME: 5–8 MINUTES | PREP TIME: 20 MINUTES | COST: $

Easy

I really don't know a simpler, more flavorful dish. Fast too—like 5 minutes. Skewering shrimp on rosemary stalks adds beautiful, subtle flavor. The sauce gets nuttiness from the butter, slivered almonds, and garlic, and then real brightness from the orange juice. I don't care if you are drinking cosmos or old-fashioneds at your cocktail party. The flavors will ring through. And please use real butter. It's a real food. Fake butter doesn't cut it, and you're not using so much when you consider that it's a sauce that gets spread over a number of shrimp. P.S. This sauce works with skewered fish, vegetables, and pork too.

1 pound large shrimp (about 16–20), shelled and deveined

1 bunch rosemary

Salt

Freshly ground pepper

Extra virgin olive oil, to brush the grill

3 tablespoons butter

2 cloves garlic, sliced

¼ cup slivered almonds

Zest and juice of 1 orange

1. Preheat a grill or grill pan to medium-high.

2. Skewer the shrimp on the rosemary stalks. Season generously with salt and pepper. Brush the grill with olive oil and grill the shrimp until cooked through and pink, about 2½ minutes per side.

3. In a pan over medium-high heat, melt the butter and then add the garlic, almonds, and orange zest and juice. Add some of the rosemary, stir, and pour over the shrimp to serve.

Baked Brie Bites

SERVES 9 | COOK TIME: 20–25 MINUTES | PREP TIME: 25–30 MINUTES | COST: $

Moderate

People have been serving baked brie for as long as they have been brie-ing and baking. My cocktail party twist is finger-food friendly. It doesn't get all gooey in your fingers, and adding some candied walnuts to the brie inside these pastry bundles is simply divine.

1 package puff pastry, thawed

½ pound Brie

1 cup Candied Walnuts (recipe follows), chopped

1 egg, beaten

1. Preheat the oven to 350 °F.

2. Roll out the puff pastry and cut into 3-inch squares. Cut the Brie into bite-sized pieces. Place a piece of Brie in the center of each puff pastry square, and top with the chopped candied walnuts. Pinch the opposite corners closed to form a package. Brush with the egg wash, and bake until golden brown, about 10–12 minutes.

Candied Walnuts

2 tablespoons unsalted butter

2 cups raw unsalted walnut halves

2 tablespoons firmly packed brown sugar

2 tablespoons granulated sugar

½ teaspoon cayenne pepper

⅛ teaspoon cinnamon

1 teaspoon sea salt

1. In a heavy skillet, cook the butter and nuts over medium heat, being careful not to burn. Stir frequently for about 1–2 minutes. In a separate bowl, combine the sugars and spices. Pour the spice mixture into the skillet, continue to stir, and cook, about 8 minutes, until the sugar is caramelized. Spread the nuts on a foil-lined sheet tray and cool completely. Store in an air-tight container at room temperature for up to two weeks.

CLINTON'S CRAFT CORNER

Tip:

Entertaining is a huge part of my life, and making my own decor ranks up there with cooking my own food. There's nothing more fun than having somebody over for a dinner party, or just over to watch a movie or for game night, and having them say, "Oh, I love those cool lanterns," and you get to say, "I made that!"

Once again, like so much in my life, home crafts take me back to the things I made in childhood, using the most inexpensive materials to make pretty things. It's kind of like six-year-old Clinton stepping in to lend a hand at a grown-up dinner.

I think we can make the same argument for why people like scratch decor the way they like homemade meals. It's something that's invested with your personality, and no matter how much money you spend, you can't buy that.

Butterscotch Truffles

SERVES 15 | COOK TIME: 30 MINUTES | PREP TIME: 30 MINUTES

INACTIVE PREP TIME: 20–30 MINUTES | COST: $

Moderate

The truffle was originally chocolate ganache covered in chocolate. Pretty darn good too. My little twist is to hide a ball of homemade butterscotch in the center. For all of you wondering what is so Scottish about butterscotch, the answer is: no one knows. What I do know is that way back when, it was advertised as something to rub on the chest in wintertime. I'm not sold. What I am sold on is finishing the truffles in sea salt because there are few things better on earth than salted caramel. Can I get an amen?

Cooking spray, for the baking pan

¼ cup water

1 cup granulated sugar

½ cup brown sugar

¼ cup light corn syrup

1 cup heavy whipping cream

4 tablespoons butter

1 teaspoon vanilla extract

1 teaspoon kosher salt

2 cups chocolate

Flaked sea salt, for sprinkling

1. Line an 8-inch square baking pan with parchment paper, letting the ends hang over the sides (for easy removal later), and then spray evenly with cooking spray.
2. Combine the water, sugars, and corn syrup in a medium saucepot. Bring to a boil over medium-high heat and cook until the mixture turns an amber color.
3. Meanwhile, in a second saucepot, combine the cream, butter, vanilla, and kosher salt, and heat over a medium heat. Once the mixture reaches a simmer, remove from the heat and set aside.
4. When the sugar mixture is golden, turn off the heat and slowly add the cream mixture to the sugar mixture. It will bubble, so be careful.
5. Turn the heat back on and continue cooking until the mixture reaches 245 °F on a candy thermometer. If your mixture becomes any hotter, the candy will be too firm. Pour out the mixture into the prepared pan and pop in the fridge for a few hours to cool. Once firm, turn the butterscotch out onto a cutting board. Remove parchment. Cut the butterscotch into 1-inch-long pieces, lengthwise. Roll into logs, and then cut ¾-inch pieces. Roll into balls.

6. Line a sheet tray with parchment paper. Melt the chocolate in the microwave or in a double boiler, and using two forks, dip the butterscotch balls into the chocolate and then place them on the sheet tray. Sprinkle with the flaked sea salt.

7. Once all the butterscotch is dipped, place in the fridge. When the chocolate is set, the truffles are ready to eat.

REVERSE MARTINI | CLINTON'S CRAFT CORNER: A CORKING GOOD IDEA | STEAK HOUSE BACON WITH GRILLED SPRING ONIONS | FAIL-SAFE PRIME RIB | ONION FLOWER POWER | CREAMED SPINACH | BOSTON CREAM PIE

PARTY LIKE IT'S YOUR BIRTHDAY!

"**YOUR BIRTHDAY IS YOUR SPECIAL DAY** out of 365 days a year, so you should set the tone and, if you want, the menu too. If you're twelve and you want to eat cereal for dinner, then the whole family should eat cereal on your twelfth birthday. Or if you want grilled cheese sandwiches and that's your favorite food, then you should be able to have grilled cheese sandwiches.

I'm not a big birthday person myself. I don't really care about my birthday all that much, 'cause I treat every day like **I'M THE MOST SPECIAL PERSON** in the world. Well actually, there is one special thing I like: my grandmother's pear crunch pie is a must. Gotta have it!

I ask you, *Chew* Crew, what is your favorite birthday meal?"

—Clinton

"**I LIKE TO PUT ON A SUIT AND TIE** (yes, I actually own some) and go someplace special. I'm all about classic dining experiences at great restaurants. But for a family meal, at home my wife and sons make something simple that I like. It could be as easy as a turkey burger, or a nice steak, seared, grilled, and finished with a little balsamic vinegar. The real key to the success of my birthday is that my wife always makes an orange sunshine birthday cake. It's kind of like a chiffon cake with an orange buttercream and segments of mandarin oranges and strawberries. Yeah, they are completely out of season in September, but we still love it, because it's our tradition. As long as she makes that cake, we know that all is right with the world."

—Mario

"**AS A GROWN-UP,** I have to be honest, I usually go out to dinner for my birthday! Mario and I share the same birthday, so this year we went to dinner at one of New York's fanciest restaurants—Mario even had to shine his Crocs. We had all the great old-school dishes, including Dover sole and whole roasted duck.

I usually cook for Lizzie on her birthday. She loves seafood and prefers a more Greek-style preparation of fish: a whole roast fish with olive oil and oregano and a nice crisp salad. She was born in March, so you don't have those beautiful summer vegetables yet, so I cook down some greens with the whole fish."

—Michael

WHEN IT COMES TO BIRTHDAY DINNER, I'm just looking for the basic sort of food that makes me happy to my core—it's the simple, straightforward, and delicious flavors that just surprise you in the easiest ways. For my birthday meal, I'd begin with a huge green leafy salad with a tart, lemony dressing and a gorgeous French baguette with fresh salted butter. Then I want chicken and dumplings. I want delicious chicken stock, great chicken thighs in there, and a moist, dense dumpling. Dessert is a toss-up. I either want a German chocolate cake because I'm a huge fan of coconut pecan icing (I would actually just prefer the icing really), or, even more simple, give me a brownie à la mode. To drink, I'd start with a cava or prosecco cocktail with a splash of elderflower, then a Spanish or Portuguese white, maybe a Vinho Verde or the wine we had at our wedding, a cold crisp Albariño.

—Daphne

BEING FROM THE MIDWEST, my husband, Matthew, loves meat and potatoes, so I do him a big steak, probably a rib eye or something as fatty and yummy and delicious. I always get it from a butcher if possible, the best I can afford. And, of course, there are potatoes too, but to make the potato a little different, maybe I'll go with a sweet potato, with an herby, salty crust and *mucho* butter.

As for my special day, well, first off, I don't want to make my own dinner; I want somebody to cook for me. I like to eat bits and bobs, a little bit of this, a little bit of that… I don't wanna commit. I just want a little bit of everything. I would be perfectly happy with lots of sides like some stuffing. Or, now that I'm away from the South, you could make a bean stew with collards and some hot water corn bread on the side, and keep the vegetables coming, and I would be totally happy.

Then I'd want dessert, say, apple pie or some kind of berry cobbler with ice cream, or an ice cream sundae with salted caramel or pistachio with some hot fudge and whipped cream and toasted nuts and a cherry top, but not that funky red cherry, a real marinated maraschino. Now you've got me thinking. I could also go for a mascarpone mousse over berries with some crumbled amaretti cookies on top. I guess I'd have to make the desserts—Matthew doesn't make desserts, but he can buy the ice cream.

—Carla

Reverse Martini

SERVES 1 | PREP TIME: 2 MINUTES | COST: $

Easy

Speaking of birthdays, we made this for Julia Child's one hundredth birthday. In the years since martinis first became popular in the 1920s, the amount of gin in them has gone way up and the amount of vermouth has kind of shrunk to a wisp, if that. Julia was not from the dry martini crowd. In fact, you could say she was from the very wet martini crowd. She liked hers with two parts vermouth to one part gin. Like foie gras and pig's feet, I guess it's an acquired taste. By the way, please note that I said gin, not vodka. Nowadays, anything clear in a glass is liable to be called a martini, but to Julia or to the Don Draper crowd, martinis were made with gin.

2½ ounces dry vermouth

¾ ounce gin

Crushed ice

1. Shake the vermouth and gin in a cocktail shaker filled with ice. Strain into a small wine glass filled with crushed ice.

Jamika Pessoa joins the *Chew* crew for a birthday bonanza!

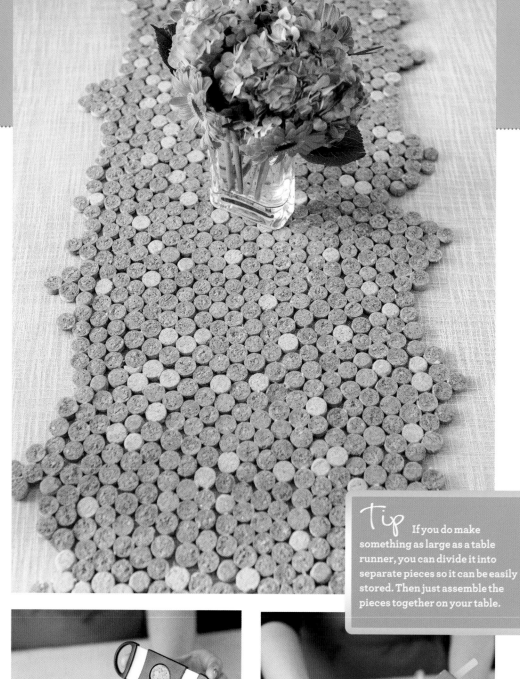

Tip If you do make something as large as a table runner, you can divide it into separate pieces so it can be easily stored. Then just assemble the pieces together on your table.

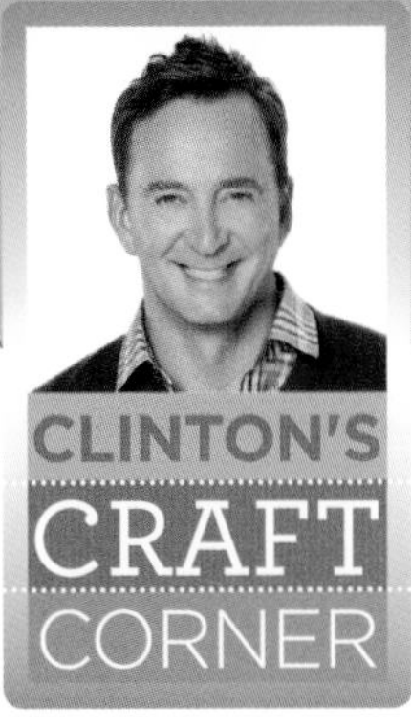

A corking good idea

As anyone who has watched more than one episode of *The Chew* knows, I am very pro-wine. Then the question becomes: What do I do with all these corks? As far as I am concerned, old corks are a new, inexpensive decorating opportunity. Here's how to use those leftover corks to make a beautiful table runner, placemats, or coasters, depending on how many corks you have.

WHAT YOU NEED

Cigar cutter or utility knife

Wine corks (use ones you already have or get them at a craft store)

Hot glue gun

HOW TO MAKE IT

1. Using a cigar cutter or utility knife, cut your corks into four or five pieces, keeping the size of each piece consistent.

2. Lay the cork pieces out, gluing them together at the sides. Be sure to keep the glue even so that everything lays flat.

3. If you'd like to add color, you can also soak your corks overnight in any leftover red wine before assembling.

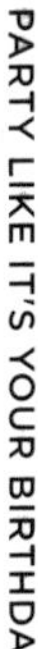

Steak House Bacon with Grilled Spring Onions

SERVES 6 TO 8 | COOK TIME: 25–30 MINUTES | PREP TIME: 15 MINUTES | COST: $

Easy

When you talk about aromas you love, nothing beats the smell of bacon. Coffee comes in as a close second, but the smell of bacon says "happy times." I know that most of you reading this agree with me, because according to research, the average American eats 18 pounds of bacon a year. Think of this dish as super thick slices of bacon or super thin smoked pork belly. Either way, it has big flavor, so it goes with a super big flavored sauce.

1 pound slab bacon

4 spring onions or scallions, sliced in half lengthwise, roots intact

Olive oil, for drizzling

Kosher salt

Freshly ground black pepper

FOR THE HOMEMADE STEAK SAUCE

2 cups balsamic vinegar

2 tablespoons red wine vinegar

1 onion, chopped

1 cup raisins

6 cloves garlic

2 anchovies

¼ cup brown sugar

1 tablespoon cumin seeds, toasted

1 tablespoon whole cloves

1 tablespoon celery seed

2 cups tomato puree

1. Preheat a grill pan to high heat.

2. Cut the slab bacon into thick slices—just shy of an inch. Arrange on the grill pan and cook until the bacon is crispy on both sides, about 3 minutes per side. Transfer to paper towel–lined plate.

3. Drizzle the spring onions lightly with olive oil, then generously season with salt and pepper and toss to coat. Grill until bright green, tender, and charred in spots, about 3 minutes.

TO MAKE THE HOMEMADE STEAK SAUCE

4. Add all the ingredients to a large saucepan and bring to a simmer. Cook until reduced by two-thirds, about 10 minutes. Strain the mixture, pressing on the solids to get maximum flavor. Discard the solids.

5. Serve the bacon with the steak sauce and spring onions.

Fail-Safe Prime Rib

SERVES 8 TO 10 | COOK TIME: 2 HOURS | PREP TIME: 10 MINUTES

INACTIVE COOK TIME: 24 HOURS | COST: $$

Moderate

A lot of people stress about making something that sounds as grand as prime rib. Don't. First of all, remember that a big cut of meat is more forgiving than a small cut. There's a bigger window of opportunity when the meat is in the right temperature range. Better yet, get an instant-read thermometer. That's the only fail-safe method I know. If the recipe book says an hour or 2 hours or whatever, that's just a rough guide. When it gets to be a half hour or 20 minutes from the time it should be done, check it. Every piece of meat is different. For medium rare, take it out of the oven at 120 °F and let it stand for 20 minutes. It will be perfect, and it goes perfectly with grated beets and horseradish. It's a slightly spicy, slightly sweet condiment that cuts the fattiness of the meat beautifully.

- 1 4-bone prime rib, bones removed and reserved
- 4 teaspoons kosher salt
- Freshly ground black pepper
- 4 sprigs fresh rosemary
- 4 cloves garlic, smashed
- 4 whole beets, red or golden
- 4 ounces arugula
- 2 teaspoons extra virgin olive oil
- 2 cups Horseradish Beets (recipe follows)

1. Liberally season the prime rib with the salt and some pepper and refrigerate overnight. An hour before cooking, remove the roast from the refrigerator to allow it to come to room temperature.

2. Meanwhile, preheat the oven to 400 °F. Put the reserved ribs in a roasting pan bowed-side up. Roast the bones for about 30 minutes.

3. Remove the pan from the oven, put the rosemary sprigs on top of the bones, and then top with the meat. The ribs will be acting as the roasting rack. Put the garlic in the bottom of the pan with the trimmings. Toss in the beets, baste with the fat, and season with salt and pepper. Baste the beef with the fat drippings and return the pan to the oven. Cook for 30 minutes and then baste the roast again.

4. Reduce the heat to 350 °F and cook until the meat is medium rare (an internal temperature of 120–125 °F), about 1 hour and 15 minutes. Keep basting the roast every 30 minutes until it is done. Keep in mind that the roast will continue to cook while resting.

5. Remove the roast from the oven and put it on a cutting board to rest, uncovered, for 20 minutes. Slice the prime rib to the desired thickness, slice the whole beets, and garnish with the arugula, olive oil, and Horseradish Beets.

FOR THE HORSERADISH BEETS

- 4 large golden beets
- 4 ounces fresh grated or prepared horseradish
- ¼ cup sherry vinegar
- 2 tablespoons extra virgin olive oil
- 2 tablespoons Dijon mustard
- Zest and juice of 1 orange
- 2 tablespoons honey
- Large pinch of kosher salt

TO MAKE THE HORSERADISH BEETS

1. Peel the beets and grate into a large bowl. Add the rest of the ingredients and toss to combine. Adjust the seasoning and serve with the prime rib.

Racked and right

Instead of using a roasting rack, I have the butcher separate the rib eye from the bones. Then I use the bones as a roasting rack. For many people, that is the choicest part of the whole prime rib. It is a lot of fun to gnaw on.

Onion Flower Power

SERVES 4 | COOK TIME: 5–7 MINUTES | PREP TIME: 20 MINUTES | COST: $

Moderate

Michael is right about people loving bacon (even vegetarians probably do in a window-shopping kind of way). I think it's just as true that people love deep-fried onion rings—so sweet, so crispy, so salty! The blooming onion that you see in restaurants is nothing more than a super jumbo fried onion. It looks really special. Just the thing to kick off a meal or as a side with a steak or pork chops.

FOR THE ONION

- Vegetable oil, for deep-frying
- 1 sweet Vidalia onion, peeled
- 1 cup flour
- 1 teaspoon sweet paprika
- 1 teaspoon cayenne
- 1 teaspoon oregano
- Salt, to taste
- 1 cup milk
- 3 eggs

FOR THE SPICY THOUSAND ISLAND DRESSING

- ½ cup mayo
- ¼ cup ketchup
- 1 tablespoon Thai chili hot sauce
- 1 tablespoon honey

TO MAKE THE ONION

1. Heat a large Dutch oven filled with oil two-thirds of the way up the sides to 360 °F.

2. Slice off the top end of the onion, leaving the root end attached. Place cut side down and begin slicing from the root down to the board, about 16 even slices around the onion, leaving the root attached.

3. Mix the flour and spices in a baking dish. Whisk the milk and eggs in another baking dish.

4. Carefully dip the onion into the flour mixture, making sure to get some inside the layers (you can also sift the seasoned flour over the entire onion), then dip into the egg mixture, and finish with the flour. Place in the oil and fry for about 5–7 minutes, until golden brown. Remove to paper towel–lined plate and season with salt.

TO MAKE THE SPICY THOUSAND ISLAND DRESSING

5. Place all the ingredients in a large bowl. Whisk together and serve alongside the onion!

Creamed Spinach

SERVES 6 | COOK TIME: 8–10 MINUTES | PREP TIME: 10 MINUTES | COST: $

Easy

One of my favorite songs from *Fiddler on the Roof* is "Tradition," and there is nothing more traditional than my favorite side: creamed spinach. I have it twice a year, so there is no reason to be shy about the butter. Bring it on! Cream too. Hey, you only have a birthday once a year.

Salt

2 pounds fresh baby spinach

1 cup whole milk

1 cup heavy cream

1 medium onion, finely chopped

½ cup (1 stick) butter

Freshly cracked black pepper

1 clove garlic, minced

½ cup flour

½ teaspoon freshly grated nutmeg

2 dashes hot sauce

1. Bring a large pot of water to a boil. Season generously with salt. Blanch the spinach for about 1–2 minutes, or until tender. Place in a fine mesh strainer, pressing to release all the liquid. Chop the spinach and set aside.

2. In a saucepan, heat the milk and cream until it's hot, but not boiling.

3. In a separate, large saucepan, over medium heat, sauté the onion in the butter until translucent. Season with salt and pepper. Add the garlic and continue sautéing, 1 more minute. Add the flour and whisk until the roux is light golden in color. Slowly whisk in the warmed milk and cream. When fully incorporated, add the nutmeg, hot sauce, and spinach, and season with salt and pepper to taste.

PARTY LIKE IT'S YOUR BIRTHDAY!

Boston Cream Pie

SERVES 10 TO 12 | COOK TIME: 35 MINUTES | PREP TIME: 40 MINUTES | COST: $

Easy

Keeping with the theme of traditional dishes, here's my take on the official dessert of the state of Massachusetts: the Boston Cream Pie, originally invented at the Parker House Hotel. That's the same place that gave us the Parker House roll. If you're keeping score, New York's famous Waldorf Astoria only has the Waldorf salad. Way to go, Boston! I give mine a little Carla twist by infusing the cream with hints of rosemary and orange. Happy birthday!

FOR THE YELLOW CAKE

- 2 large eggs, plus 2 large egg yolks
- 2 teaspoons vanilla extract
- ⅓ cup buttermilk
- 1¾ cups all-purpose flour, sifted, measured, and then sifted again
- 1 cup granulated sugar
- 1¾ teaspoons baking powder
- ½ teaspoon salt
- 4 tablespoons unsalted butter, softened
- ⅓ cup canola oil
- ½ cup heavy cream, whipped to soft peaks

FOR THE ROSEMARY ORANGE PASTRY CREAM

- 1 cup whole milk
- 1 cup heavy cream
- 1 sprig rosemary
- 4–5 2-inch strips orange peel (note: use a peeler)

TO MAKE THE YELLOW CAKE

1. Preheat the oven to 325 °F.
2. In a large liquid measuring cup, combine the eggs and vanilla with 2 tablespoons of the buttermilk.
3. In a large mixing bowl, combine the flour, sugar, baking powder, and salt, whisking well.
4. With the hand mixer on medium-low, beat in the butter, canola oil, and the remaining buttermilk into the dry mixture. Stir in the egg mixture in three parts, while scraping down the sides of the mixing bowl. Do not overmix. Fold the whipped cream into the batter.
5. Spoon the batter into three prepared cake pans. Bang the pans on the counter to release any air bubbles. Place in the oven and bake for 25–30 minutes, or until the top springs back and the cake starts to pull away from the sides of the pan.
6. Let cool for 10 minutes on a wire rack, then turn out to cool completely on the rack before frosting.

TO MAKE THE ROSEMARY ORANGE PASTRY CREAM

7. In a stainless steel pot, steam the milk and cream with the rosemary and orange peel.

½ cup sugar

¼ cup cornstarch

Pinch of fine salt

4 egg yolks

2 tablespoons butter

FOR THE DARK CHOCOLATE GLAZE WITH ORANGE LIQUEUR

9 ounces bittersweet chocolate

2 tablespoons butter

½ cup heavy cream

1–2 tablespoons triple sec

8. Combine the sugar, cornstarch, and salt in a bowl. Pour the hot milk mixture into the bowl and whisk to combine. Return the milk mixture to the pot and bring to a low boil, continuing to whisk.

9. In another bowl, whisk the egg yolks and temper ½ cup of the hot milk mixture into the eggs. Gradually pour this back into the pot and continue to whisk as the mixture comes to a boil. Continue to cook until thick, about 3 more minutes. It should coat the back of a spoon but should not clump.

10. Strain through a fine mesh strainer into a clean bowl with the pats of butter in the bottom. Stir until the butter melts. Chill with plastic wrap directly on top of the cream.

TO MAKE THE DARK CHOCOLATE GLAZE WITH ORANGE LIQUEUR

11. Put the chocolate and butter into a heatproof bowl. Heat the heavy cream and triple sec until just hot. Pour the hot cream over the chocolate and butter, and stir until smooth. Let cool slightly before pouring over the cake.

TO MAKE THE BOSTON CREAM PIE

12. Layer the cakes and the pastry cream. Drizzle the chocolate glaze over the top of the cake, just enough so the sides of the cake aren't covered completely.

PARTYING WITH THE KIDS

"**HEY, WHILE WE ARE ON THE SUBJECT OF BIRTHDAY PARTIES**, let's not forget the kids. I think for a lot of kids, burgers and hot dogs are the way to go, but when my son, Kyle, was growing up, we had to go a little esoteric because he is allergic to red meat. Thankfully he loves spicy food, so it wasn't hard. Typically we'd do Asian-themed meals. He loved pot stickers, so we'd do different-themed pot stickers or maybe Indian samosas, but they would typically have an Asian slant for his kind of meals. More generally, there isn't anything more American than the sandwich, and you can do so many different themes on sandwiches that kids really love—eggplant parmigiana or meatballs come to mind. Or you can get a bunch of cold cuts and pickles and condiments, some good hero rolls, and let the kids invent their own sandwiches. And then there is the pizza party: this is handy in my family, where we have thirteen nephews and two nieces, mostly under twelve years old. So I make a pizza dough that I grill outside and put out the toppings, and the kids pick and choose their own custom pizzas. Mostly they go for simple stuff: tomato sauce, fresh mozzarella, sometimes pepperoni. Some of them are going through the phase where they want nothing green, so god forbid you should put some basil out there! Long story short, birthday parties are a great way for us grown-ups to show the youngsters that good food can be fun food too."

—Michael

Bug Juice

SERVES 8 | COOK TIME: 5 MINUTES | PREP TIME: 15 MINUTES | COST: $

Easy

Anyone who ever went to summer camp probably remembers bug juice. It was usually powdered fruit punch and water. Some people say it got its name because it was so sweet even the bugs stayed away. I like the little herbal taste you get when you steep a sprig of thyme in it. Now that you're a grown-up and you're not in summer camp anymore, you can always add some spirits to it—I recommend vodka!

1 cup sugar

1½ cups water

1 bunch thyme

2 pints raspberries, plus more to garnish

2 cups lemon juice

Seltzer

Lime slices, to garnish

Ice

1. In a small saucepot over medium-high heat, combine the sugar, water, and thyme to make the simple syrup.

2. Pulse the raspberries in a food processor until smooth. Strain the pureed mixture.

3. In a large pitcher, combine the raspberry puree with the lemon juice and 1–2 cups of the simple syrup, depending on the desired level of sweetness.

4. Top the pitcher with seltzer. Stir to mix, and garnish with raspberries and lime slices. Serve over ice.

Shaved Ice

SERVES 8 | COOK TIME: 10 MINUTES | PREP TIME: 10 MINUTES | COST: $

Easy

What could be better than strolling down the boardwalk on a hot summer day after you've won your stuffed teddy bear? Topping it off with a cooling and refreshing shaved ice. Even if you can't get to the beach, you can still have shaved ice at home, and my bet is that you're not going to get anything as nutritious as my fresh-fruit version. Try it with a few different fruits, and let the kids choose what they want.

1 pound pitted frozen or fresh cherries, thawed and drained with the juice reserved

¼ cup lemon juice

¼ cup water

½ cup sugar

Shaved or crushed ice

1. In a blender or food processor, puree the cherries.
2. In a saucepan over medium heat, add the cherry puree, lemon juice, water, and sugar. Bring to a boil and reduce by half, about 3–4 minutes. Remove from the heat, and strain the sauce through a sieve. Allow to cool before use.
3. Drizzle over shaved or crushed ice.

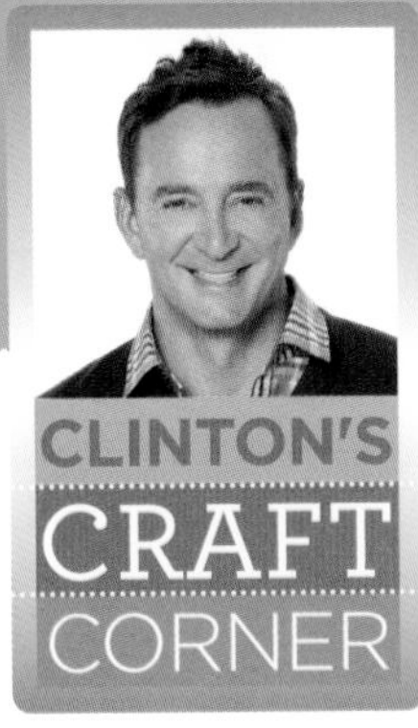

Knock the stuffing out piñata

I've yet to meet the kid who didn't love a piñata. In fact, you can add grown-ups to the legions of piñata lovers. I guess it's because we all love surprises and want to know what's inside, especially when the inside is full of treats. I don't know why it works out this way, but as each kid takes a whack at the piñata, it never seems to want to break until the shrimpiest kid picks up the stick, smacks the piñata, and out pour the goodies. You have to love that!

WHAT YOU NEED

- Flour
- Water
- Salt
- Large balloon
- Newspaper, cut into 2-inch strips
- 4 packages of colored tissue paper
- Colored construction paper
- Craft glue
- String, to hang the piñata

HOW TO MAKE IT

1. Combine equal parts flour and water. Add a generous pinch of salt and whisk until smooth. (The salt prevents your papier-mâché from growing mold.)

2. Inflate and tie off the balloon. Rest the balloon on an empty jar or bowl.

3. Dip the newspaper strips into the flour and water mixture, wiping off any excess. Lay the strips over the balloon, making sure all the pieces lay smoothly on the surface. (Be sure to leave a hole for filling with candy.) Once the balloon is completely covered, allow to dry. Continue this process until the entire balloon has been covered with 3–4 layers.

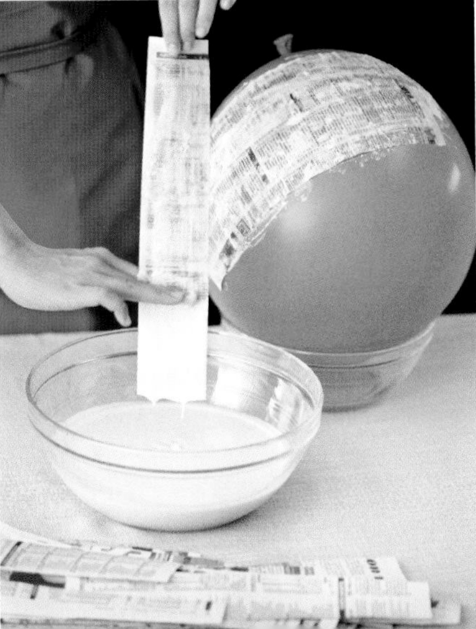

4. Allow the papier-mâché to dry completely. Once it has dried, pop the balloon and remove it from the interior of the piñata.

5. Cut your tissue paper into squares and crumple them to give them volume. Using craft glue, stick them to your papier-mâché in your desired design. From construction paper or other craft supplies, make and attach eyes, ears, feet, or any other features your creature may have.

6. Once it has been decorated, punch a small hole on either side and pull a string through to use to hang your piñata.

7. Finally, fill with candy, and it is ready for your celebration!

Sloppy Joes

SERVES 8 | COOK TIME: 40 MINUTES | PREP TIME: 15 MINUTES | COST: $

Easy

This recipe comes from my son Leo and was in a cookbook that he and his brother, Benno, gave me for my fiftieth birthday. When I am on the road in the summer, my boys have a Batali Boys Cookoff contest pretty much every night, and this is one of their creations. Now here I am—a big shot Iron Chef—and the most popular Batali recipe is my kids'! What's up with that? It's very cool. Of course, I had to add my own little twists, which are some beer for flavor (the alcohol cooks out) and some jalapeños for a spicy kick. I've looked and looked, in search of who this guy Joe was. No luck. But I know where the "sloppy" part of the name comes from: there's no way you can eat these without squishing some of the meat on you, usually on a piece of clothing where it really shows up well.

FOR THE PICO DE GALLO

3 tomatoes, chopped
1 jalapeño, minced
½ red onion, minced
¼ cup cilantro, chopped
Salt
Pepper
Juice of 1 lime

FOR THE SLOPPY JOES

2 tablespoons vegetable oil
1 onion, diced
1 jalapeño, sliced
1 pound ground round
2 tablespoons sugar
5 tablespoons tomato paste
½ 12-ounce beer
8 hamburger rolls

TO MAKE THE PICO DE GALLO

1. Mix all the ingredients together and set aside.

TO MAKE THE SLOPPY JOES

2. Place a skillet over medium-high heat and let it get hot for about a minute.
3. Add the oil and spread it so it covers the bottom of the pan. Add the onion and jalapeño.
4. Add the ground round and cook, breaking up the meat with the back of a spoon, until all the pink is gone, about 15 minutes.
5. Add the sugar, tomato paste, and beer, and combine.
6. When the liquid starts to simmer, reduce the heat to low, partially cover, and simmer for 25 minutes. Stir occasionally to keep the bottom from scorching.
7. Open the rolls and arrange them on a plate. Spoon the meat mixture over it, top with a spoonful of pico de gallo, and serve.

Mock Chicken

SERVES 8 | COOK TIME: 8 TO 10 MINUTES | PREP TIME: 20 MINUTES

INACTIVE PREP TIME: 30 MINUTES | COST: $

Easy

Usually when I see the word *mock* in a recipe, you lose me, because it often means tofu with a lot of sauce that you hope will fool people into thinking they're eating chicken. Never fear! When a Batali makes mock chicken, he is going to use pork and veal. Actually, I should say "she," because this is a recipe my mom picked up at a neighbor's, and it became one of our household favorites. Why is it called chicken if it's made with pork and veal? Because my mom liked to squeeze the meat on the skewers so they looked like chicken legs (at least to her). They're crispy, crunchy, meaty, and well seasoned. Kids love them.

Skewers
1 pound pork shoulder
1 sleeve saltine crackers
3 eggs, lightly beaten
Flour, for dredging
Salt
Pepper
3 tablespoons extra virgin olive oil
3 tablespoons butter
2 tablespoons vermouth (optional)
Lemon wedges, for garnish

1. Soak the skewers in water for 30 minutes.
2. Cut the pork shoulder into chicken-finger-sized pieces (about 1-inch cubes).
3. Crush the saltine crackers and place into a shallow dish. Put the lightly beaten eggs into another shallow dish. Have a third dish with flour for dredging.
4. Insert the skewers into the pieces of pork as to resemble a chicken drumstick.
5. Season each "drumstick" on both sides with salt and pepper.
6. Preheat the oven to 400 °F.
7. Heat the olive oil and butter in a skillet over medium-high heat. Once smoking, dip each "drumstick" into the flour, the egg, then dredge in the cracker crumbs.

Mario's mom, Marilyn, shows the crew how Mock Chicken is done!

8. Panfry each piece lightly on both sides, then, if desired, deglaze the pan with the vermouth. Once all the pieces have been fried, transfer to a baking sheet and place in the oven to finish cooking, about 8–10 minutes. Allow to cool before serving. Garnish with a squeeze of lemon juice from the wedges.

Homemade Twinkies

SERVES 12 | COOK TIME: 15 MINUTES | PREP TIME: 30 MINUTES | COST: $

Moderate

When I heard that Hostess, purveyors of the legendary Twinkie, might be going out of business, I did what any self-respecting chef would do. Did I pick up a pen and write my congressman? Did I organize like-minded Twinkie true believers to go picket my supermarket? No way! I decided to figure out my own Twinkie recipe. These have that buttery, creamy Twinkie-ness that we all love, but I actually think these are better. Not because Twinkies aren't great, but homemade is always the way I roll.

FOR THE CAKES

- Nonstick cooking spray or vegetable oil
- ½ cup cake flour
- ¼ cup all-purpose flour
- 1 teaspoon baking powder
- ½ teaspoon salt
- 2 tablespoons milk
- 4 tablespoons unsalted butter
- 1 teaspoon vanilla extract
- 5 large eggs, separated (room temperature)
- ¾ cup granulated sugar
- ⅓ teaspoon cream of tartar

TO MAKE THE CAKES

1. Preheat the oven to 350 °F. Adjust the oven rack to the lower-middle position.

2. Spray Twinkie molds with nonstick cooking spray or grease with vegetable oil.

3. In a mixing bowl, whisk together the cake flour, all-purpose flour, baking powder, and salt. In a small saucepan over low heat, heat the milk and butter until the butter melts. Remove from the heat and add the vanilla. Cover to keep warm.

4. In the bowl of a stand mixer, beat the egg whites on high speed until foamy. Gradually add 6 tablespoons of the sugar and the cream of tartar, and continue to beat until the whites reach soft peaks, about 6 minutes.

5. Transfer the beaten egg whites to a large bowl and add the egg yolks to the standing mixer bowl (there's no need to clean the bowl). Beat the egg yolks with the remaining 6 tablespoons of sugar on medium-high speed, until the mixture is very thick and a pale lemon color, about 5 minutes. Add the beaten egg whites to the yolks, but do not mix.

FOR THE FILLING

6 tablespoons unsalted butter (room temperature)

1½ cups confectioners' sugar

½ teaspoon vanilla extract

½ teaspoon salt

¾ cup marshmallow fluff

2 tablespoons heavy cream

2 tablespoons condensed milk

SPECIAL EQUIPMENT

twinkie molds

6. Sprinkle the flour mixture over the egg whites and then mix everything on low speed for just 10 seconds. Remove the bowl from the mixer, make a well in the center of the batter, and pour the melted butter mixture into the well. Fold gently with a large rubber spatula until the batter shows no trace of flour and the whites and yolks are evenly mixed, about 8 strokes.

7. Immediately scrape the batter into the prepared molds, filling each with about ¾ cup of the batter (a measuring cup can aid in this process). Bake until the cake tops are light brown and feel firm and spring back when touched, 13–15 minutes. Transfer the pan containing the molds to a wire rack and allow the cakes to cool in the molds.

TO MAKE THE FILLING

8. In the bowl of a stand mixer, beat together the butter, confectioners' sugar, vanilla extract, salt, and marshmallow fluff. Add the cream and condensed milk, and beat just until smooth. Transfer the frosting to a pastry bag fitted with a ¼-inch round tip. Pipe frosting into three spots on the underside of the Twinkie, taking care not to overfill. Serve while still warm.

Peach Maple Sherbet Sandwiches

SERVES 8 | COOK TIME: 15 MINUTES | PREP TIME: 20 MINUTES

INACTIVE COOK TIME: 2 HOURS | COST: $

Easy

The only thing I like better than dessert is a dessert made with 100 percent natural, unprocessed ingredients. These sandwiches are so healthy that they make you wonder, "Could they possibly be delicious too?" The answer will become clear to you after you put out a tray of them for the kids at a birthday party.

FOR THE COOKIES

1½ cups whole wheat flour, plus extra flour for dusting

½ cup ground oats

½ teaspoon salt

½ teaspoon cinnamon

½–¾ cup coconut oil

¼ cup maple syrup

½ teaspoon vanilla

FOR THE SHERBET

3 cups fresh or frozen peaches

1⅓ cups almond milk, plus more if needed

2 tablespoons maple syrup

TO MAKE THE COOKIES

1. In a medium bowl, combine all the dry ingredients. Slowly add the coconut oil and maple syrup, mixing to combine. Finish with the vanilla. Form into a disk and place in the refrigerator for 30 minutes.

2. Preheat the oven to 350 °F.

3. Lightly dust a cutting board or counter with flour and roll the dough out to ¼ inch thick. Using a cookie cutter, cut out 3-inch rounds. Place on a parchment-lined baking sheet. Bake for 15–20 minutes. Allow the cookies to cool.

TO MAKE THE SHERBET

4. Using a blender, combine the sherbet ingredients and blend until smooth. Pour into a freezer-safe container and freeze for 2 hours or until set.

5. When ready to assemble the sandwiches, remove the sherbet from the freezer and take out of the container. Using the same cookie cutter as used with the dough, cut through the sherbet to make equal-sized cylinders. Next, slice the sherbet and sandwich each slice in between two cookies. Arrange the sandwiches on a sheet tray and refreeze until set.

CRANBERRY FIZZ | BRUSCHETTA WITH PEAS AND RICOTTA | VEGETABLE CAPONATA ON SWEET POTATO CRISPS | SWORDFISH PICCATA WITH ESCAROLE SALAD | CLINTON'S CRAFT CORNER: THE UPCYCLED TABLETOP | PAN-SEARED SALMON WITH BEET SALAD | DOUBLE-CUT PORK CHOPS WITH CORN AND JALAPEÑO SALAD | BEEF TENDERLOIN WITH POMEGRANATE FENNEL SALAD | RED WINE–BRAISED SHORT RIBS | ARTICHOKE SCAFATA | CROWN ROAST OF LAMB WITH QUINOA STUFFING AND BLACK TRUFFLE GRATIN | PEAR TARTE TATIN | CHOCOLATE PUMPKIN CAKE |

SATURDAY NIGHT SPECIALS

"**SITTING AROUND THE TABLE ON SATURDAY NIGHT,** sharing a glass of wine with friends, for me is the "Ahhhhh" moment; it makes the whole week worthwhile. Saturday night dinner is the sparkly carrot at the end of the stick that is my exhausting workweek. But I'm not too exhausted to cook or accessorize my table. It's the day when I want to make that special meal for special people. I mean, who invites people they really don't care about a lot for **SATURDAY NIGHT DINNER?** And on Saturday, even with the errands of weekly shopping and dry cleaning drop-off, there's enough time to devote to doing it up. Sunday, I don't feel that way, maybe because the daily grind starts again the next day. I feel that on Saturdays, you should **"LIVE IT UP, BECAUSE THERE'S NO TOMORROW."** Occasionally this leads to living it up so much that tomorrow lets me know I've overdone it. Hey, so what? Enjoy your Saturday."

—Clinton

Cranberry Fizz

SERVES 6 | COOK TIME: 5–10 MINUTES | PREP TIME: 2 MINUTES | COST: $

Easy

I came up with this in the Clinton Kelly Cocktail Research Institute, also known as my dressing room. I was looking for another way to get cranberries into a Thanksgiving menu, but it's so good I refuse to wait around all year to kick back and drink one, or two, or whatever. Extra bonus point: it's pretty.

½ lemon

½ orange, plus slices for garnish

Ice

2 cups gin

2 cups cranberry juice

2 cups club soda

Cranberries, for garnish

1. Cut the lemon into 4 wedges and the orange into 4 slices. Place the lemon and orange slices into a pint glass. Muddle aggressively.

2. Transfer the lemon and orange mixture to a pitcher and fill with ice. Add the gin, and then top with cranberry juice and soda. Stir. Garnish with the cranberries and orange slices.

Bruschetta with Peas and Ricotta

SERVES 8 | COOK TIME: 2–5 MINTUES | PREP TIME: 5 MINUTES | COST: $

Easy

Simple, but if the peas are fresh and local, the flavor is wow! That's because they are sweet and tender and haven't had time to turn starchy the way peas that were trucked in from far away often are. If spring peas have a best friend, it's mint. They just want to be served together. And since the flavors are so fresh and delicate, creamy and slightly sweet ricotta pulls it all together.

4 cups peas, shelled

Kosher salt

2 cups fresh sheep's milk ricotta cheese

Zest of 1 lemon

½ cup grated Parmesan

¼ cup fresh mint leaves

Freshly ground black pepper

¼ cup extra virgin olive oil

½ baguette, cut into slices at a bias

1. Fill a large bowl with ice and water. Add the peas to a well-salted, large pot of boiling water. Make sure there is way more water than peas and enough salt for it to taste like the ocean. Cook the peas for about 30 seconds. Remove the peas to the ice bath.
2. In a food processor, mix the ricotta, lemon zest, Parmesan, and mint.
3. Drain the peas and add them to the food processor. Pulse just until the mixture comes together—you want to keep a little texture and not make it totally smooth.
4. Spoon the mixture into a serving bowl, crack some black pepper over the top, and drizzle with extra virgin olive oil.
5. Heat a grill pan to medium-high. Brush the pieces of bread with olive oil and season with salt and pepper. Grill on each side until crisp and grill marks appear, about 1–2 minutes per side.
6. Serve each crostini topped with the pea mixture.

Vegetable Caponata on Sweet Potato Crisps

SERVES 6 | COOK TIME: 20–25 MINUTES | PREP TIME: 15 MINUTES | COST: $

Moderate

Everybody should have some caponata around. It's a traditional Sicilian sweet-and-sour cooked vegetable medley that serves as a halfway house between a vegetable and a condiment. It's a wonderful appetizer on crostini, or served alongside fish or a roast. I made this on the show with Fran Drescher, who really knows her onions when it comes to food, and she can cut veggies in my kitchen anytime. We're talking grown-up knife skills. My twist here is serving it on crisp sweet potato cakes that get that lacy, crunchy, crinkly crust like you achieve with potato pancakes (one of Fran's family's favorites). The secret is hot oil.

FOR THE CAPONATA

4 tablespoons olive oil

½ cup onion, cut into ¼-inch dice

½ cup celery root, cut into ¼-inch dice

½ cup fennel, cut into ¼-inch dice and reserving the fennel fronds

½ cup sweet potato, cut into ¼-inch dice

Salt

Pepper

¼ cup apple cider vinegar

¼ cup water

2 tablespoons fresh mint, chopped

FOR THE SWEET POTATO CAKES

2 cups sweet potatoes, peeled and grated

½ cup rice flour

TO MAKE THE CAPONATA

1. In a large cast-iron skillet over medium-high heat, add the olive oil. Sauté the onion for 1–2 minutes, until soft and slightly caramelized. Add the remaining vegetables and season with salt and pepper. Cook for about 10–15 minutes, stirring occasionally.

2. Once the vegetables are caramelized and soft, deglaze with the vinegar and water, and reduce until all the liquid has evaporated. Adjust the seasoning, and, off the heat, stir in the mint.

TO MAKE THE SWEET POTATO CAKES

3. In a large mixing bowl, combine all the sweet potato cake ingredients. Season with salt and pepper.

4. In another cast-iron skillet, over medium-high heat, add about 3 tablespoons of olive oil. Once hot, use a tablespoon measure and scoop heaping tablespoons of the sweet potato mixture and press in the pan. The thickness should be about ¼ inch. It may be necessary to work in batches, depending on the size of the pan. Cook the crisps for 3–4 minutes on each side, or until golden brown.

⅓ cup almond milk

2 tablespoons cocoa powder

2 teaspoons ground cumin

Salt

Pepper

Olive oil, for frying

5. Once the sweet potato crisps are cooked through, remove to a plate lined with paper towels. Place on a platter and top the sweet potato crisps with the caponata and garnish with the fennel fronds.

Swordfish Piccata with Escarole Salad

SERVES 4 | COOK TIME: 10 MINUTES | PREP TIME: 15 MINUTES | COST: $

Moderate

I went to college in New Jersey and I am a huge fan of everything in New Jersey, from Bruce Springsteen to beefsteak tomatoes. The license plates say it's THE GARDEN STATE, but to me it's also THE OCEAN STATE, with wonderful seafood from its rich waters. Jersey swordfish is a particular favorite—it's big on flavor, which is why I like it with a quick, easy, and super flavorful pan sauce. When I want to add flavor, I think of salt, acidity, and heat—spicy heat, in this case, with the famous Bomba peppers of Calabria. They pack a punch, so they want big flavors to balance them. I look to add flavor in every step in this dish, so instead of dredging in flour, I use pulverized almonds, which give you the crispiness of flour and an extra sweet layer of flavor. The same holds true for the escarole salad—big flavor, starting out with crushed anchovies. When I made this on the show with Daisy Fuentes, she gave me her philosophy on salad dressing—and love: "Salads, like people, are best underdressed."

Works for me.

FOR THE SWORDFISH PICCATA

4 1-inch-thick swordfish steaks, skin removed

Salt, to taste

Pepper, to taste

1 cup almond flour or ground almonds

2 tablespoons extra virgin olive oil

¼ cup dry white wine

2 tablespoons butter

Zest and juice of 2 lemons

1½ tablespoons Bomba Calabrese or red pepper paste

2 tablespoons capers, drained

2 tablespoons fresh parsley leaves, plus more for garnish

TO MAKE THE SWORDFISH PICCATA

1. Season the fish with salt and pepper. Place the almond flour or ground almonds in a baking dish and season with salt and pepper. Dredge the fish on all sides in the flour, patting off any excess.

2. In a large skillet, heat the olive oil over high heat until it just begins to smoke. Cook the fish in hot oil, flipping once to brown both sides, about 3 minutes per side. Work in batches if necessary to avoid overcrowding the pan. Remove the fish to a paper towel–lined plate.

A fishy secret

Many people are fearful of cooking fish. Don't be one of them. The secret is, don't overcook it. Overcooking is how you get that unpleasant "fishy" flavor. Moist and flaky is the way to go.

FOR THE ESCAROLE SALAD

3 anchovy fillets packed in oil, chopped to a paste

Zest and juice of 2 lemons

1 clove garlic, minced

2 tablespoons extra virgin olive oil

2 tablespoons red wine vinegar

1 head of escarole, washed and torn

3. Keeping the pan over medium heat, add the wine, butter, lemon zest and juice, and Bomba Calabrese to the pan. Toss in the capers and parsley, and season with salt and pepper, cooking just to combine flavors, about 1 minute. Plate the fish and top with the pan sauce. Garnish with the parsley and serve with the escarole salad.

TO MAKE THE ESCAROLE SALAD

4. Combine the anchovies, lemon zest and juice, and garlic in a medium bowl. Whisk in the olive oil and red wine vinegar, and toss the dressing with the escarole leaves to coat. Season with salt and pepper to taste.

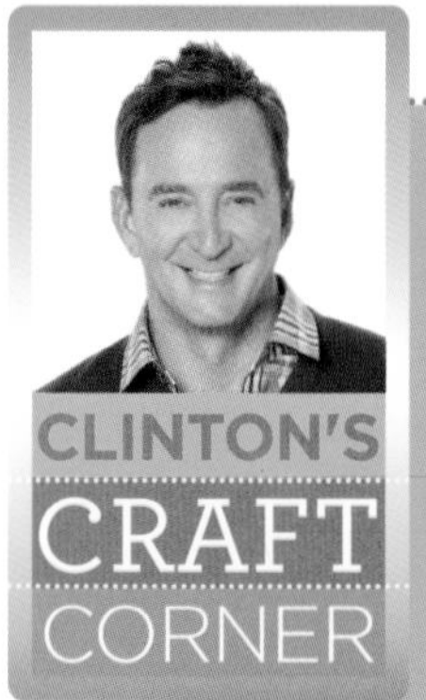

The upcycled tabletop

Tablecloths can be pricey. You are also limited to what the designers like. That may not always be what you like. Hey, why not roll your own? Cloth from the fabric store is very inexpensive (remnants are even cheaper), and the choices are endless. For serving trays, I like to rummage around garage sales for antique mirrors; they really dress up a table (and make it look like you have twice as much food!). And here's my numero uno tip: make friends with your florist and stop by at the end of the day and ask about any leftover flowers that didn't sell. They're always still beautiful and a real bargain.

Pan-Seared Salmon with Beet Salad

SERVES 4 | COOK TIME: 7–10 MINUTES | COST: $

Easy

Fish is a lot more fun when you get the skin nice and crispy. Even for professionals, I find that a nonstick pan is the most foolproof way to crisp up fish. Just make sure the skin is dry before you put it in the pan. When you give salmon this treatment, it is beautifully full of flavor, which means it can stand up to beets, horseradish, lemon juice, and mustard. These flavors open up the palate and are totally satisfying. If you are weight-conscious (who isn't these days?), do like I do and skip the starch side dish. This is a satisfying meal all by itself.

- 3 tablespoons extra virgin olive oil
- 4 5-ounce skin-on salmon fillets
- Salt, to taste
- Pepper, to taste
- 1 tablespoon mustard
- Juice of ½ lemon, plus more for garnish
- 1 large beet, peeled and grated
- 1 tablespoon fresh horseradish, peeled and grated
- ¼ cup fresh parsley, leaves torn
- 3 scallions, sliced on a bias

1. Heat a large cast-iron skillet over medium-high heat with 2 tablespoons of the olive oil. Season the salmon with salt and pepper.
2. Cook the salmon skin side down for 3–4 minutes, making sure the skin is crispy. Flip the salmon and continue to cook for 3 minutes, for medium rare, or until the salmon reaches desired doneness.
3. Meanwhile, in a medium bowl, whisk together the remaining oil, mustard, and lemon juice. Toss in the remaining ingredients to coat lightly, and season with salt and pepper.
4. Plate the salmon skin side up with the beet salad. Garnish with the lemon juice.

Hold your horses!

This recipe calls for grating fresh horseradish. Chances are you should be able to find it in your town. I live in Cleveland, which is what they call a "mid-market" town. The way I figure it, if I can find it here, it's a good bet you can find it in most places. If not, prepared horseradish packs a punch too.

Double-Cut Pork Chops with Corn and Jalapeño Salad

SERVES 4 TO 6 | COOK TIME: 17–20 MINUTES | PREP TIME: 15 MINUTES
INACTIVE PREP TIME: 2–24 HOURS | COST: $

Moderate

When you see the words *pork chops* in the name of a recipe, you think that's what it's all about. Not really. For me it starts with the corn salad. When corn is sweet and just picked, this spicy, herby salad really excites me—crunchy, smoky, and fiery. I can eat it with pork chops or chicken or fish . . . don't let me forget shrimp. As for the pork chops, here's my main rule, and it holds true for everything I grill: set up your grill so that one side is very hot and the other side is a lower heat; you char it up to start and move it to the cool side to cook more gently and evenly all the way through.

FOR THE PORK CHOPS

- 1 tablespoon sugar
- 1 tablespoon salt
- 1 tablespoon coriander, toasted and ground
- 4 double-cut pork chops
- 2 tablespoons olive oil, plus more to drizzle

FOR THE CORN AND JALAPEÑO SALAD

- 4 ears corn, shucked, with silk removed
- Zest and juice of 2 limes
- ¼ cup cilantro (leaves only), chopped
- 1 pint Sweet 100 tomatoes, halved
- 3 scallions, chopped
- 1 clove garlic, minced
- 1 jalapeño, minced
- Freshly ground black pepper

TO MAKE THE PORK CHOPS

1. Combine the sugar, salt, and coriander.
2. Rub each of the pork chops on both sides with the mixture, and refrigerate for 2 hours and up to overnight.
3. Preheat half the grill to high, and preheat the other half to low heat.
4. Drizzle the chops with olive oil and grill for 3–4 minutes per side over high heat, to sear. Once seared, transfer to the cooler part of the grill to finish cooking through, about 10 minutes, or until medium to medium well.

TO MAKE THE CORN AND JALAPEÑO SALAD

5. Grill the ears of corn till charred at parts, about 3 minutes per side. Remove the kernels from the ears to a bowl, and toss with the lime zest and juice, cilantro, tomatoes, scallions, garlic, and jalapeño. Add the 2 tablespoons of olive oil and toss to coat. Season with salt and pepper.
6. Serve the pork chops sliced and topped with the salad.

Beef Tenderloin with Pomegranate Fennel Salad

SERVES 8 | COOK TIME: 35–45 MINUTES | PREP TIME: 20 MINUTES | COST: $$

Moderate

CLINTON: Carla, Daphne, and I put our heads together to make something special for Michael and Mario. And let this be a lesson to you about cooking for "serious" food people. Don't be intimidated: if it's good, it doesn't have to be complicated. And always remember that guys like them got in the chef business in the first place because they love food.

CARLA: Amen, sir. And we wanted to do something that was Mediterranean in spirit and in honor of Michael and Mario, so we have fennel, oranges, a rub full of herbs, lots of olive oil, and pomegranate syrup. And instead of using a roasting rack, we lay the roast right on the vegetables so that they cook in all the juices from the roast.

DAPHNE: Which got me thinking. Those vegetables and fruits are wonderful cooked, but they'd also make a great salad. That way you really explore all the texture and flavor possibilities of these ingredients.

FOR THE RUB

- 2 teaspoons ground fennel seed
- 1 teaspoon freshly cracked black pepper
- 3 tablespoons olive oil
- 2 teaspoons kosher salt
- 2 tablespoons rosemary, finely chopped, plus sprigs for garnish

FOR THE BEEF TENDERLOIN

- 3 pounds beef tenderloin tied with butcher's twine
- 2 fennel stalks, cut into 3-inch pieces with bulbs and fronds reserved
- 2 sprigs thyme, plus more for garnish

TO MAKE THE BEEF TENDERLOIN

1. Preheat the oven to 375 °F.

2. In a small bowl, mix together the ingredients for the rub, making a loose paste. Rub the tied tenderloin thoroughly with the mixture.

3. In a medium-sized bowl, toss together the fennel stalks, thyme sprigs, and orange slices. Drizzle generously with the olive oil, and season with salt and pepper. Add these to the bottom of a roasting pan, spreading evenly. Place the tenderloin on top of the fennel orange mixture. Place the roasting pan in the oven and cook until an instant-read thermometer reads 125 °F (for medium rare), about 30–40 minutes.

4. Remove the tenderloin from the pan and cut the twine off. Let rest at least 10 minutes. Transfer the vegetables to a serving platter. Garnish with the fresh rosemary sprigs.

1 orange, sliced into rounds ¼ inch thick

3 tablespoons olive oil

Salt, to taste

Pepper, to taste

1 cup red wine

½ cup beef stock

¼ cup pomegranate syrup

2 tablespoons butter

FOR THE POMEGRANATE FENNEL SALAD

Zest and segments of 1 orange, separated

Juice of 2 lemons

2 tablespoons olive oil

Salt

Pepper

½ cup pomegranate seeds

5. Place the roasting rack on the stove over medium heat. Add the wine and, with a wooden spoon, scrape up the bits on the bottom of the pan. Once the wine has reduced by half, add the beef stock and pomegranate syrup. Reduce only slightly, 1–2 minutes. Whisk in the butter. Pour the sauce into a gravy boat.

TO MAKE THE POMEGRANATE FENNEL SALAD

6. Shave the reserved fennel bulbs thinly into a bowl of ice water. In a small mixing bowl, whisk the orange zest, lemon juice, and about 2 tablespoons of olive oil together, and season with salt and pepper.

7. Drain the fennel well right before serving. Toss the fennel with the orange segments and coat everything in the vinaigrette. Mix in the pomegranate seeds. Plate and garnish with the reserved fennel fronds.

8. To serve, slice the tenderloin into medallions. Place some of the sauce onto a plate and top with a piece or two of beef. Top with a little of the salad.

Red Wine–Braised Short Ribs

SERVES 8 TO 10 | COOK TIME: 1 HOUR 30 MINUTES | PREP TIME: 20 MINUTES

COST: $$

Moderate

Short ribs are a true one-pot wonder. There's no comfort food that is more comforting than the aromas of slow-cooking wine-soaked beef filling up your pad. When you make it this way, it tastes so truly luxurious that you forget it's an inexpensive cut. What I love is the ease of this recipe: you cook your aromatic vegetables down, add some wine and whatever, put it in the oven at a low temperature, and voilà, a delicious dinner is ready in an hour.

6 pounds bone-in beef short ribs

Kosher salt

Freshly ground black pepper

4 tablespoons olive oil

2 stalks celery, diced

1 medium carrot, diced

1 onion, diced

6 cloves garlic

1 Fresno chili, halved

¼ cup tomato paste

5 sprigs fresh thyme (leaves only)

1 bay leaf

1 quart chicken stock

2 cups dry red wine

⅓ cup red wine vinegar

1. Season the short ribs with salt and pepper and set aside.

2. Preheat the oven to 325 °F.

3. Heat 2 tablespoons of the olive oil in a large enameled cast-iron Dutch oven over medium-high heat. Add half of the short ribs to the pan and cook on all sides until browned, about 2 minutes per side. Transfer the ribs to a plate. Repeat with the remaining ribs.

4. Pour off all but 2 or 3 tablespoons of fat from the pan. Add the celery, carrot, onion, garlic, and chili to the pan, along with a large pinch of salt, and cook over medium heat until softened, about 7 minutes. Add the tomato paste and cook, stirring, until glossy, about 2 minutes. Add the thyme sprigs and bay leaf, and cook, stirring, for 2 minutes. Scrape the bottom of the pan. Add the stock, wine, and vinegar, and bring to a boil. Return the short ribs to the pan, cover, and braise in the oven for 1 hour.

5. Remove the ribs to a serving platter and cover to keep warm while you simmer the liquid to reduce it by half. Pour the sauce over the ribs and top them with the Watercress Salad.

FOR THE WATERCRESS SALAD

1 bunch watercress, cleaned and stemmed

1 tablespoon fresh horseradish, grated, plus more for garnish

2 teaspoons chives, chopped

1 tablespoon red wine vinegar

Drizzle of olive oil, to taste

Salt, to taste

Pepper, to taste

TO MAKE THE WATERCRESS SALAD

6. Combine all the ingredients in a bowl. Serve on top of the braised short ribs. If you want, add a grating of horseradish over the completed dish before serving

NOTE: You can also use brisket or top round for this dish.

To braise a beast

The key to braising is not to drown the meat in liquid. You only want the liquid to come about three-quarters of the way up the meat so that it caramelizes while it braises.

Artichoke Scafata

SERVES 4 TO 6 | **COOK TIME: 15–20 MINUTES** | **PREP TIME: 20 MINUTES** | **COST: $**

Moderate

If you had to ask me for one dish that looks like spring, here's my vote. There's a good reason for that: it's the kind of thing that Romans make in the spring. What's their recipe? Basically you go to the market, find the things that look like they just came out of the ground, bring them home, put them in a big pot, and cook them up. There's no getting around the fact that artichokes require a little more prep time and practice than other vegetables, and, at least in the American diet, they are kind of special, so why not have them on that special day, as in Saturday, when you get down to serious cooking?

2 small lemons, halved, plus juice to garnish

15 baby artichokes

¼ cup extra virgin olive oil, plus more to garnish

1 red onion, thinly sliced

1 teaspoon hot red pepper flakes

½ cup dry white wine

1 pound fresh peas, shelled

4 bunches scallions, root ends trimmed and whites and greens cut into 2-inch pieces

Salt, to taste

Freshly ground pepper, to taste

1 bunch fresh mint leaves

1. Fill a large bowl with water, and squeeze the lemon halves into it.

2. Remove and discard the tough outer leaves of the artichokes, and trim the stems. Then cut the artichokes in half and scoop out the choke. As you work, submerge the halved artichokes in the lemon water.

3. In a Dutch oven, heat the olive oil over medium heat until hot, add the onion and cook until soft and translucent, about 4 minutes. Add the red pepper flakes, the wine, 1 cup of hot water, the peas, and the drained artichokes. Cover, and cook until the artichokes are just tender, 10–12 minutes. Add the scallions, cover, and reduce the heat to a simmer. Cook until the scallions are wilted and soft, about 4 minutes. Season with salt and black pepper.

4. Tear the mint leaves into pieces and sprinkle them over the scafata. Garnish with a drizzle of olive oil and lemon juice. Serve either warm or at room temperature.

Crown Roast of Lamb with Quinoa Stuffing and Black Truffle Gratin

SERVES 8 | COOK TIME: 35 TO 45 MINUTES | PREP TIME: 20 MINUTES | COST: $$

Moderate

MARIO: This special dinner has a naughty and nice side. I made the naughty side dish with potato gratin and black truffles.

DAPHNE: Naughty just like you. I'm making a nice side of quinoa, almonds, pomegranate, and honey, proving that to be nice, you don't have to be flavorless. And quinoa is chock-full of nice health benefits.

MARIO: Just like you, Daph.

DAPHNE: Touché, chef. Very often stuffing is heavy and loaded with fat and calories, but this one is quite simple and based on quinoa. It's a beautiful grain, full of protein and minerals and easy to cook.

MARIO: I always think of naughty as taking longer than nice, but watching you make this...maybe not. My naughty side starts with a cream and Parmigiano-Reggiano sauce laced with nutmeg and Swiss cheese. And now the totally amazing black truffles. They're big-time naughty. When pigs and hounds dig them out of the dirt, they think they are following the aroma of a sex-starved lady pig or dog.

DAPHNE: Enough with the naughty, or we'll end up doing *The Chew* on the Spice Channel.

MARIO: And don't let me forget the succulent, full-flavored, fresh-off-the-hoof crown roast of lamb. Couldn't be simpler: season, put in the oven, and take a nap for 20 minutes.

DAPHNE: Now that's my idea of nice.

MARIO: But naughty if you oversleep!

FOR THE CROWN ROAST

1 2-pound crown roast of lamb (have your butcher prepare it for you)

Salt, to taste

Pepper, to taste

4 tablespoons extra virgin olive oil

TO MAKE THE CROWN ROAST

1. Preheat the oven to 400 °F.

2. Season the lamb with a generous amount of salt and pepper, drizzle with the olive oil, and set aside at room temperature.

FOR THE QUINOA STUFFING

3 tablespoons extra virgin olive oil

2 shallots, sliced

2 cloves garlic, minced

3 cups quinoa, cooked according to package instructions

Zest and juice of 3 lemons

¼ cup slivered almonds, toasted

½ cup fresh mint leaves, chiffonade

TO MAKE THE QUINOA STUFFING

3. Heat a skillet over medium-high heat with 2 tablespoons of the olive oil. Sauté the shallots and garlic just until tender, about 2–3 minutes. In a large bowl, mix the cooked quinoa, lemon zest and juice, shallots and garlic mixture, almonds, mint, coriander, and pomegranate seeds. Drizzle with the remaining olive oil and honey, and season with salt and pepper. Toss to combine.

4. In a large roasting pan, make a bed for the roast to sit on with a few large spoonfuls of the quinoa stuffing. Transfer the lamb roast to the bed and fill with the remaining quinoa mix. Drizzle with a little extra virgin olive oil and place in the preheated oven. Roast the lamb until the internal temperature reaches 130 °F, approximately 20–30 minutes.

2 teaspoons ground coriander

½ cup pomegranate seeds

1 tablespoon honey

Salt, to taste

Pepper, to taste

FOR THE YOGURT SAUCE

1 cup strained yogurt

Zest and juice of 1 lemon

1 clove garlic, minced

1 handful of picked mint leaves, chopped

Salt and pepper, to taste

Olive oil, to taste

5. Remove from the oven and transfer to a large platter. Top with the quinoa mix from the pan. Loosely tent with aluminum foil and allow to rest for 10 minutes before serving with the yogurt sauce.

TO MAKE THE YOGURT SAUCE

6. In a food processor, combine the ingredients and pulse until smooth. Continue to puree while drizzling the olive oil. Taste and adjust to desired seasoning.

Rinse and repeat

If you rinse your quinoa thoroughly, it gets rid of that bitter taste that some people notice.

FOR THE BLACK TRUFFLE GRATIN

Butter, for the baking dish

2 pounds Yukon Gold potatoes, peeled and sliced crosswise into ⅛-inch-thick slices

Salt, to taste

Pepper, to taste

3 cups heavy cream

¾ cup grated Parmigiano-Reggiano

¼ teaspoon freshly grated nutmeg

1 small black truffle, plus more for garnish (optional)

¾ cup grated Emmentaler or good-quality Swiss cheese

TO MAKE THE BLACK TRUFFLE GRATIN

1. Place a rack in the middle of the oven and preheat to 400 °F.

2. Generously butter a gratin dish or other shallow baking dish. Layer potatoes in the casserole dish. Season with salt and pepper.

3. Put the cream in a heavy-bottomed pan and bring to a simmer. Simmer for about 5 minutes. Stir in the Parmigiano-Reggiano and grate the nutmeg and half the truffle, if using. Season the cream generously with salt and pepper.

4. Carefully pour the cream on top of the potatoes and sprinkle on the Emmentaler or Swiss cheese. Grate more truffle on top and season with more pepper.

5. Bake in the oven until the top is a deep golden brown, about 40 minutes, or until a toothpick inserted into the potatoes comes out without resistance. Let the potatoes cool slightly (this will help thicken the cream and set the gratin) for at least 20 minutes.

6. Serve the potatoes and grate fresh black truffles over each serving. Serve with the lamb.

Pear Tarte Tatin

SERVES 6 | COOK TIME: 35–40 MINUTES | PREP TIME: 10 MINUTES | COST: $

Easy

An excellent and easy dessert, provided you have one of two things: 1.) homemade puff pastry, or 2.) a good store-bought puff pastry, which means it's made with flour and real butter, and that's it. To get that real French pastry shop tatin-y taste, browned butter and sugar give a beautiful caramel color and flavor. Then caramelizing the pears in the pan will give them a super tasteful crust.

4 tablespoons butter

½ cup sugar

1 teaspoon salt

4–5 ripe and firm pears, peeled, cored, and halved lengthwise

3 tablespoons flour

1 package puff pastry, thawed

Vanilla ice cream, to serve

1. Preheat the oven to 375 °F.
2. In a large ovenproof sauté pan, melt the butter over medium-high heat. Once bubbling, sprinkle in the sugar and the salt.
3. Add the pears to the pan cut side down. Cook until the sugar begins to turn light golden brown, about 3 minutes. Flip the pears and cook for another 30 seconds.
4. Dust the counter with flour and roll out the puff pastry to the size of the sauté pan. Top the sauté pan with the puff pastry, tucking the edges into the pan.
5. Transfer to the oven and cook for 25–30 minutes, or until the pastry is golden brown. Let the tarte rest for about 5 minutes to cool enough to handle.
6. Place the serving side of a larger flat platter over the pan. The platter should be larger than the pan. Carefully flip the platter and pan to reveal the tarte. Serve with vanilla ice cream.

Chocolate Pumpkin Cake

SERVES 10 | COOK TIME: 35–45 MINUTES | PREP TIME: 45 MINUTES | COST: $

Moderate

I know many of you have never been completely sold on pumpkin as a dessert. It's just that pumpkins are so big you have to do as many things as you can with the pumpkin in the interests of keeping it out of the compost heap. So someone said, "Hey, let's convince people it's a great dessert too." This moist, sweet, creamy, chocolate-covered cake will make it hard to believe that pumpkin was ever used for anything besides dessert.

FOR THE PUMPKIN CAKE

2 cups sugar

1 cup vegetable oil

4 large eggs

2 cups all-purpose flour

2 teaspoons baking soda

1 teaspoon baking powder

3 teaspoons pumpkin pie spice

1 teaspoon salt

2 cups fresh or canned pumpkin puree (see Note page 113)

FOR THE MASCARPONE FILLING

2 cups mascarpone

1 cup fresh or canned pumpkin puree, strained of excess liquid

1 tablespoon pumpkin pie spice

2 teaspoons salt

4 cups powdered sugar

1 teaspoon vanilla extract

TO MAKE THE PUMPKIN CAKE

1. Preheat the oven to 350 °F. Grease and flour two 9-inch round layer cake pans.

2. Combine the sugar, vegetable oil, and eggs in a large mixing bowl, and mix well. Whisk the dry ingredients in a separate bowl. Stir the dry into the wet ingredients until just combined. Fold in the pumpkin puree.

3. Divide the batter between the two cake pans. Bake for 35–40 minutes, rotating the pans halfway through cooking. When a toothpick comes out clean, the cakes are done. Let cool for 5 minutes, and then turn the cakes out onto cooling racks.

TO MAKE THE MASCARPONE FILLING

4. While the cakes are cooling, make the filling. Beat the mascarpone and the pumpkin puree until blended, and then add the pumpkin spice, salt, and powdered sugar. Mix at a high speed until blended, about 1 minute. Once it's fully combined, add the vanilla and beat for another 30 seconds.

5. Once the cakes have cooled completely, cut through each cake horizontally with a serrated knife (there will now be four rounds of cake to work with).

FOR THE DARK CHOCOLATE GANACHE

3 tablespoons corn syrup

6 ounces heavy cream

12 ounces dark chocolate, chopped into small bits

½ teaspoon vanilla extract

Ginger snaps, crushed, for garnish

6. Spread the filling evenly between the layers.

7. Once assembled, transfer the cake to a cake stand with parchment paper lined around the edges (to keep the cake stand clean).

TO MAKE THE DARK CHOCOLATE GANACHE

8. In a small saucepan, combine the corn syrup and heavy cream, and bring to a simmer. Add the chocolate. Stir until smooth. Remove from the heat and add the vanilla extract.

9. Pour over the cake and use a spoon or butter knife to make sure that all of the cake is covered in chocolate.

10. Garnish with the ginger snaps. Once the ganache is set, remove the parchment. Slice and serve.

GINGER PEACH MARGARITA | GRILLED CORN SOUP WITH BASIL AND FETA | LOBSTER THERMIDOR | LOVE LETTERS (VEGETABLES, PASTA, AND CHEESE, FROM ITALY WITH LOVE) | GRILLED T-BONE LAMB CHOPS WITH FAVA BEAN AND FETA SALAD | MANGO BONBONS

DATE NIGHT!

YOU'VE HEARD IT A MILLION TIMES: the way to a man's heart is through his stomach. I think the same thing goes for a woman's heart as well. A woman likes to be cooked for. I think there's a different kind of meal that you put together for a first date, or a third date, or a fourth for that matter. I would never cook an elaborate meal on a first date. Face it, that's a lot of time investment for somebody who might turn out to be a nut job. But if it's for someone you care about, then time or even money isn't the object. **YOU SPEND FOR THE BEST YOU CAN AFFORD** and you make it the best you can. In this case, it's the thought—the sentiment behind the meal—that really counts.

So, guys, what makes for a good date night dinner in your book?

—Clinton

"I LIKE DINNER FOR TWO at the house, as opposed to a "romantic" expensive date. Since you're not blowing a car payment at a restaurant, you can spend a little more on the ingredients and you are still going to come out ahead and make something swanky. An old warhorse like beef Wellington may sound like a tired dish, but if you get really nice beef and get really good puff pastry and get some really good liver, you can make something really remarkable out of it. The key thing is getting the best ingredients—get to know the butchers and produce guys, even at supermarkets. If you take the time to talk with them, you are going to get VIP treatment, especially when they see that you're a regular customer, and that's true for all retail.

Now think about the wine you two will have at home. You probably rarely spend $35 for a bottle at home, but in a restaurant that's far from the most expensive wine on the list, and sometimes it's the cheapest. Look at it this way: that $35 bottle at home would cost $140 in a restaurant. Sounds like a deal, don't you think? Same goes for the beef Wellington. At $25 per person, you've got something that would easily cost twice that in a good restaurant. So stay home for your date. It's cheaper and you won't have to ask, "My place or yours?""

—Mario

"WHEN IT COMES TO DATE NIGHT at our house, my husband, John, and I often do a salad, but a bit fancier. I truly love a salad with sweet onions, tomato, lemon, olive oil, and feta cheese right in the dressing tossed with pomegranates and fresh field greens. And don't let me forget fish tacos. That doesn't sound that romantic, but there's nothing I love more, especially when we grill fresh fish. I often like to wing it, taking inspiration from what John is in the mood for, seeing what we have in the fridge, and taking it from there.

Really the most important thing is setting the scene. If you take the time to put out candles and flowers and set the table, it says: "This night is special for the two of us." Music too makes all the difference; I have all kinds of playlists. It depends—if we're doing old school, we'll have an Ella Fitzgerald mix. We have a great playlist that I call "boat music," because it's what I envision the Saint-Tropez yachts would play. It's sort of Brazilian, very soothing, but also kind of upbeat and lively, and now that I think about it, I don't know what it has to do with Saint-Tropez in France except, in my mind, it's all one big romantic stew.''

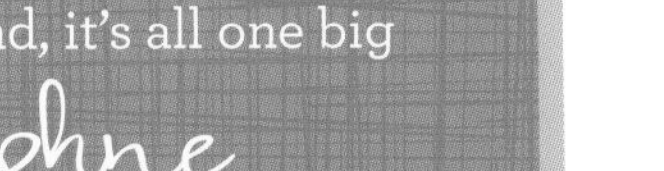

IT'S HARD TO PICK A MEAL that floats everyone's boat. Every couple is different, so my advice is more general. It's really important when cooking something special to stay in your wheelhouse. Don't go for something complicated and fancy that you've never made before. A steamed lobster or a rosy red rib eye with a nice char on the crust is simple, and both are probably at the top of everyone's wish list. Stay light instead of heavy. Nothing rivals too many heavy courses as a romantic buzzkill. Champagne is always nice, but so are plenty of less expensive sparkling wines. They all say this is a celebration. Okay, if you backed me into a corner and said, "Pick one dish right now," I might say a paella. It's a one-pot meal but full of little tastes of shellfish, sausage, and sometimes chicken. It looks amazing and most everyone likes it yet people rarely make it. Or you could always just ask your special guy or gal what they would like you to make. The important thing is that you make it. No home delivery or takeout.

—Michael

DATE NIGHT is about the other person. What makes them happy. Call it "fork play." For me that other person is my husband, Matthew. He loves Indian food, so I will often make him a curry with all kinds of special stuff on the side—chutneys, spices, nuts. I call those special little flavor packages "bits and bobs." They are the accents that make a dish special. One thing I never make is something heavy that puts him right to sleep. So if it's a long-cooked braise, it will be something intensely flavored, but it won't sit in your stomach like a sack of potatoes. I take my hat off to Michael Symon, who taught me a lot about brightening and emphasizing the flavor potential in my old standbys. It has helped me take what I already know and make it better. That's always my goal, Date Night and every day. You've got to better-up yourself.

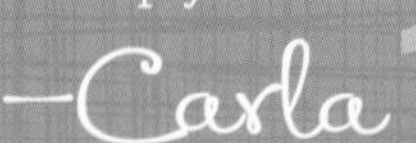

Ginger Peach Margarita

SERVES 1 | COOK TIME: 10 MINUTES | PREP TIME: 5 MINUTES | COST: $

Easy

The secret ingredient to this gringo's margarita is a ginger simple syrup. Take my advice and make enough to store in the fridge. It's great in iced tea or over ice cream. I researched this cocktail with great dedication (can I get an "Olé!" please?). So make sure you follow these measurements exactly . . . or not. You're the one who has to drink it. And buy the best tequila you can afford because, believe me, there is a difference the next morning.

1½ ounces silver tequila

¾ ounce lime juice

½ ounce peach schnapps

1 ounce peach puree

¾ ounce Ginger Simple Syrup

Ice

2 peaches, sliced

Champagne

1. Add all the ingredients except the peach slices and champagne to a shaker. Shake well and pour into a salt-rimmed margarita glass. Add a splash of champagne to the top of the margarita and serve with a slice of peach.

2. To make a frozen margarita, puree all the ingredients (except the peach slices and champagne) in a blender. Serve in a salt-rimmed glass, topped with champagne and garnished with a peach slice.

FOR THE GINGER SIMPLE SYRUP

1 cup sugar

1 cup water

1 large piece of fresh ginger, peeled and sliced into thin rounds

TO MAKE THE GINGER SIMPLE SYRUP

1. Bring the sugar and water to a boil in a saucepan over medium-high heat until the sugar dissolves. Add the ginger and bring to a simmer. Remove from the heat, and let steep for 1 hour. Pour the syrup through a sieve into an airtight container and discard the ginger. Refrigerate for up to 5 days.

Grilled Corn Soup with Basil and Feta

SERVES 4 | COOK TIME: 20–30 MINUTES | PREP TIME: 15 MINUTES | COST: $

Easy

I'm from New Jersey, the Garden State. When I was growing up, we'd all pile in the car to drive down to the Jersey Shore, and we always stopped at the farm stand for some fresh-picked corn. It was so good we'd always buy a bushel of the stuff. With apologies to Michael, who is a champion of midwestern corn, there is nothing as sweet as Jersey sweet corn. We had to find some delicious ways to use it all up, and that's where this delicious creamy corn soup comes in. It takes about 5 minutes to make, but it has deep, complex flavor. It's equally good warm or cold.

½ head garlic, skin on, plus 2 cloves

Extra virgin olive oil

4 ears corn, shucked

Salt

Freshly ground pepper

1 quart water

½ onion, chopped

2 carrots

½ cup Greek yogurt

½ cup feta, crumbled

Basil (leaves only), chiffonade, for garnish

1. Preheat the oven to 400 °F.
2. Place the garlic head on a sheet of aluminum foil, drizzle with 1 tablespoon of extra virgin olive oil, wrap with foil, and roast for 20 minutes until soft and caramelized.
3. Preheat a grill or grill pan to medium-high. Brush the grill with extra virgin olive oil. Season the corn with salt and pepper and grill, until charred lightly, about 10 minutes, rotating through the cooking process. Cut the kernels from the cob, reserving the cobs, and set aside.
4. Place the cobs into a pot, and top with the water. Add the onion, carrots, and garlic cloves, plus a pinch of salt and pepper. Bring to a boil, cover, and simmer. After 15 minutes, strain the corn stock, discarding the solids.
5. Add the charred corn, roasted garlic, and Greek yogurt to a blender with 1–2 cups of the corn stock, and blend until completely pureed. Add a little more of the corn stock to loosen the soup, if necessary. Check seasonings and adjust to taste.
6. Pour the puree into serving bowls and top with the crumbled feta. Garnish with the basil.

NOTE: Corn stock will last 3–5 days in the refrigerator and up to 6 months in the freezer.

Stock up on stock

Although this recipe calls for grilling instead of boiling corn, I always have some corn stock on hand made from water corn was boiled in. You can reduce it, freeze it in ice cube trays, and have a delicious soup base.

Lobster Thermidor

SERVES 4 | COOK TIME: 10–15 MINUTES | PREP TIME: 20 MINUTES | COST: $$

Easy

This is my numero uno D&D meal, as in decadent and delicious. I first had it when I was thirteen years old and went to the Clam Box in Carmel, California, with my grandparents, "Kona" and "Wild Bill." One taste was all it took. I thought it was the food of the gods (or, as Mario calls it, "an upscale casserole"). I try to have it once a year, for special occasions. Many thanks to Julia Child who inspired this, but I simplified it a bit. She has you put the cooked lobster back in the shells, but that takes time and effort, and when it's date night—or any night, for that matter—I want to get right down to business.

4 cooked lobster tails

1 stick unsalted butter, cut into pieces

½ onion, minced

1 teaspoon thyme

½ teaspoon paprika

¼ pound mushrooms, trimmed and thinly sliced

1 cup white wine

½ cup heavy cream

Juice of ½ lemon

¼ teaspoon black pepper

⅛ teaspoon salt

2 cups crushed crackers

1. Cut the lobster meat into small pieces.
2. In a sauté pan over medium heat, melt 1 tablespoon of the butter, then add the onion, thyme, paprika, and mushrooms, and sauté for 8 minutes. Add the lobster and toss, then set aside.
3. In a saucepot, reduce the wine by three-fourths, then whisk in the cream and reduce for another minute. Remove from the heat and stir in the remaining 7 tablespoons of butter, along with the lemon juice, pepper, and salt.
4. Preheat the broiler.
5. Place the lobster meat into ramekins, then add the cream sauce. Top with the crushed cracker mixture, then place under the broiler until golden brown, about 3–5 minutes. Serve.

Warming up with beurre

The crowning touch for Lobster Thermidor and many other seafood dishes is a simple sauce that the French call *beurre blanc*. It is made with butter, cream, and white wine. I ask you, with that combination, how can you go wrong?

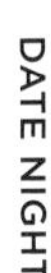

Love Letters (Vegetables, Pasta, and Cheese, from Italy with Love)

SERVES 4 TO 6 | COOK TIME: 35–40 MINUTES | PREP TIME: 45 MINUTES | COST: $

Moderate

This is a perfect meal for a first date, but don't let that stop you if the two of you are already in a long-term relationship... even married! Why not rekindle the flames of love with a little wilted chard in a ravioli? I promise it's a lot sexier than it sounds. These lovely little pasta packages have two things going for them in the date department. First, they make for nice bites instead of long strands of pasta, which can be slurpy and sloppy, and no one wants to be slurpy and sloppy when they are trying to impress a romantic interest. And second, they are something you can make together in the kitchen. Cooking compatibility is, in my book, one of the keys to a successful love affair.

FOR THE RAVIOLI

5 tablespoons olive oil

1 red onion, finely diced

1 teaspoon chili flakes

Kosher salt

3 cups chard, washed, stemmed, and thinly sliced

Freshly ground black pepper

2 cups ricotta

⅓ cup Parmigiano-Reggiano, grated

½ teaspoon freshly grated nutmeg

1 pound fresh pasta sheets or Homemade Pasta (recipe follows)

Semolina, for dusting

TO MAKE THE RAVIOLI

1. In a large sauté pan over medium-high heat, add about 3 tablespoons of the olive oil.
2. Add the onion and chili flakes and season with salt, then cook until tender, about 6–8 minutes.
3. Add the remaining olive oil and toss in the chard. Season with salt and pepper, and cook for about 20 minutes, or until the chard is tender. Remove the chard mixture into a bowl and let cool slightly.
4. Stir in the ricotta and Parmigiano-Reggiano, and season with the nutmeg, salt, and pepper.
5. Lay out a sheet of pasta, working one at a time, and cut the sheets into 3-inch squares. Place 1 tablespoon chard filling into the center of each square.
6. Wet the edges of the pasta with warm water, and fold in half to form rectangles (or love letters). Press edges to seal. Put the finished ravioli on a cookie sheet sprinkled with semolina.
7. Bring a pot of salted water to a boil.
8. Cook the ravioli 4–5 minutes.

FOR THE PASTA SAUCE

- 2 tablespoons olive oil, plus more to drizzle
- ½ pound bacon, chopped
- 1 red onion, thinly sliced
- 3 cloves garlic, thinly sliced
- 1½ teaspoons crushed red pepper
- 1 ½ cups store-bought tomato sauce
- Salt, to taste
- Pepper, to taste
- ½ cup freshly grated Parmigiano-Reggiano
- 1 large handful parsley, chopped finely

TO MAKE THE PASTA SAUCE

9. Meanwhile, in a large sauté pan over medium-high heat, add about 2 tablespoons of olive oil and cook the bacon until crisp. Add the onion and cook for about 3 minutes more. Toss in the garlic and the crushed red pepper, and cook for another minute.

10. Add about 1½ cups of tomato sauce to the pan and cook for about 5 minutes to meld the flavors. Season with salt and pepper.

11. With a slotted spoon, transfer the ravioli to the tomato sauce and toss to coat. Grate in the Parmigiano-Reggiano and a drizzle of olive oil, and toss again.

12. Plate the ravioli and top with the chopped parsley.

FOR THE HOMEMADE PASTA

- 3 or 4 large eggs
- 10 ounces all-purpose flour, plus more for dusting

TO MAKE THE HOMEMADE PASTA

1. Make a mound of flour, create a well in the middle, add 3 of the eggs, and mix with a fork, slowly incorporating the flour. (Or mix all together in a stand mixer.) If too dry, add a fourth egg yolk. If still too dry, add the white. Once the dough forms a ball, knead it for 15–20 minutes. Wrap it in plastic and let it rest for at least 30 minutes.

2. You can now cut off a portion (about a quarter) and roll it out with a pasta machine. You can also roll it out by hand, on a floured wooden board with a wooden rolling pin. Roll dough out in one direction. Flip and roll out in the other direction. Flip, turning 90 degrees, and continue. The idea is to stretch the dough until it's very thin—thin enough that you should be able to see the grains of the wooden board through the sheet.

Grilled T-Bone Lamb Chops with Fava Bean and Feta Salad

SERVES 4 | COOK TIME: 10–15 MINUTES | PREP TIME: 20 MINUTES

INACTIVE COOK TIME: 8–24 HOURS | COST: $$

Moderate

Lamb is a wonderful tradition among my ancestors in Greece. There's a reason for that: sheep, like many animals, have their babies in spring, so they have all summer and fall to put on some weight to weather the winter. Fava is one of the first crops of spring, so it's traditional to pair these two foods. You've probably noticed in restaurants that we chefs go nuts for favas for about a month. Finally! Something fresh and local! I use the T-bone for this rather than the more common chops because the bone runs all the way through, which gives it more flavor, and it's cheaper. I think there's a good lesson in this recipe: if you use prime local ingredients, you will often have more flavor and be satisfied with less. I'm good with 5 ounces of meat rather than a big ol' slab of a lesser grade.

FOR THE LAMB

2 tablespoons kosher salt

1 tablespoon coriander seed, toasted

1 teaspoon sugar

8 T-bone lamb chops

1 teaspoon red pepper flakes

Olive oil, to drizzle

TO MAKE THE LAMB

1. Put the salt, coriander seeds, and sugar into a mortar and pestle, and crush to blend. Place the lamb chops on a wire rack set over a baking sheet. Liberally season the chops on both sides with the spice blend. Sprinkle each side with the red pepper flakes. Allow to sit in the refrigerator, covered, for 8–24 hours before grilling, if possible. This will act as a quick cure, adding more flavor to the lamb when it's cooked.

2. Preheat a grill to medium-high heat.

3. Drizzle olive oil over the lamb and place on the grill, cooking until an instant-read thermometer inserted into the thickest part of the meat reaches 125–130 °F, for medium rare to medium, about 4–6 minutes per side, turning once. Allow the chops to rest briefly before serving.

FOR THE FAVA BEAN AND FETA SALAD

Salt

1 cup fava beans

1 shallot, minced

2 cloves garlic, smashed and minced

3 tablespoons red wine vinegar

½ cup extra virgin olive oil

Pinch of red pepper chili flakes

Freshly ground black pepper, to taste

¾ cup feta, crumbled

8–10 sprigs fresh mint leaves, torn

TO MAKE THE FAVA BEAN AND FETA SALAD

4. Fill a large bowl with ice and water. Place a large pot of water over high heat and bring to a boil. Add salt to taste. Add the fava beans to the water and blanch for about 40–50 seconds, or to al dente. Immediately plunge the beans into the ice bath to cool. Once cooled, remove the outer layer and set the shelled beans aside.

5. To a bowl, add the shallot and garlic, and season with salt to help bring out the moisture. Add the red wine vinegar, extra virgin olive oil, red pepper chili flakes, and freshly ground black pepper to taste. Add the shelled fava beans, crumbled feta, and torn mint leaves. Toss to combine. Taste for seasoning.

6. For each serving, place 2 lamb chops onto a plate. Top with the feta salad.

Spice up the spice

I like to buy spices whole and then roast them and grind them just before cooking with them. *Mucho mas* flavor!

Mango Bonbons

SERVES 10 | COOK TIME: 5 MINUTES | PREP TIME: 20 MINUTES

INACTIVE PREP TIME: 10 MINUTES | COST: $

Easy

Date night is special. Even better is special, cheap, and delicious. And even better than that it is low-calorie too! Okay, sports fans, how about incredibly yummy, 6 cents a serving, and 8 calories. I'd like to say this recipe came about solely through a thunderbolt of inspiration. That would be only half true. The other half is I'm kind of cheap or, to use a more refined word, *economical*. Why go out and spend umpteen dollars on expensive bonbons when you can probably make something just as good or better yourself? I know what I said about 8 calories. That's only if you eat just one. But these are so good, I'd say that's not gonna happen. Okay, so eat three. That's still only 24 calories for dessert.

¾ cup Greek yogurt
⅓ cup milk
1 cup frozen mango
2 tablespoons honey
Pinch of salt
1 cup dark chocolate
¼ cup dried mango, finely chopped (optional)

SPECIAL EQUIPMENT
truffle molds

1. Add the yogurt, milk, mango, honey, and salt to a blender, and blend until smooth.
2. Pour the mixture into a silicone bonbon mold and freeze for at least 2 hours, or until firm.
3. Heat the chocolate over a double boiler just until melted. Remove from the heat. Let the chocolate cool to room temperature, but not harden.
4. Dip each frozen bonbon in the chocolate and place on a wax paper–lined cookie sheet.
5. Sprinkle dried mango over the center of each dipped bonbon, if using.
6. Place the bonbons in the freezer to set for about 10 minutes, or until ready to serve. You can make these several days in advance.

BATTLE OF THE IRON GRANDMAS | DAISY'S CHICKEN AND DUMPLINGS | MAMA T'S SAUSAGE AND BEEF CASSEROLE | ANTOINETTE LORDO'S MELT-IN-YOUR-MOUTH MEATLOAF | SPIKED ICED TEA | THAI CHOPPED CHICKEN SALAD | ROAST CHICKEN WITH SALSA VERDE AND CREAMY POTATOES | SWAMP THING | HAM WITH HABANERO GLAZE | ITALIAN TURKEY | GREEK TURKEY | CHEESY BACON, BUTTERNUT SQUASH, MAC 'N CHEESE CASSEROLE | CLINTON'S CRAFT CORNER: A WREATH FULL OF BLESSINGS | SCALLION CHILI SWEET POTATO CAKE | CRANBERRY-APPLE COBBLER | LEMON POUND CAKE | GRILLED PINEAPPLE UPSIDE-DOWN SANDWICH | NECTARINE BLACKBERRY BUCKLE

SUNDAY SIT-DOWNS

"**MORE THAN ANY OTHER MEAL** you will ever have, you will remember those Sunday sit-downs from when you were a young child or a teenager the most. Those meals always bring back a reverie. You eat, you sit there afterward, there's chitchat, maybe somebody brings out a deck of cards or a board game. It's pretty much the one ritual that defines family. Even after parents and grandparents are gone, it's a way to bring the spirit of those you loved back among the **PEOPLE NEAREST AND DEAREST** to them. I swear, my grandmother's spirit hovers in the steam rising from the kitchen stove. So does my grandfather's as I think about the vegetables he would pick in the garden. It's a memory that feels so real, that I even see the garden dirt he always tracked in with him. If you have grandchildren, I insist that you have them sit down and **HAVE THIS MEAL** with you. It will stay with them forever and be passed down to their children for as long as the words *roast chicken, prime rib,* and *leg of lamb* are spoken."

—Clinton

"**SUNDAY DINNER** is all about family. I'm not home as often as I used to be, home being Cleveland, and it ends up being a travel day now, so when I do get the chance for Sunday dinner at home, it's a big deal. For most of my life, Sunday was the day the family got together and cooked. It was typically my mom who would do the cooking, and it was always some big-style casserole dish like moussaka or the amazing Greek Calle lasagna called pastitsio. My sister, my grandparents, everyone would come over, and we would eat."

—Michael

"**GROWING UP**, Sunday dinner in our house was always a little on the earlier side, but it was never 3 o'clock, I mean, it was 4:30 or 5, because we still had a day to enjoy. It was the one dinner during the week where you couldn't get up from the table until everyone really kind of gave it up. We always had to say, "Can I get down please?"

During football season, the day revolves around the games. I like to make food you can put on before the first game, check between the two games, and then eat after the second game (but before Sunday night football). The TV has to go off during all suppers—in and out of football season—maybe there's a little music in the background, but it's no TV, no cell phones, no text messaging, and no tweets. You eat, you talk. That's the whole deal." —Mario

“**SUNDAY DINNER** is not usually a big event at our house. We usually entertain Saturday night for cocktails/dinner or Sunday late morning for brunch. Sunday nights are the time John and I reserve for each other—we either go out or order in, or we cook a simpler meal that doesn't take much prep or cleanup. (I do like to cook my make-and-store meals for the week ahead during the day on Sunday—but I want the evening to relax and recharge for the week ahead.) Sometimes, if we're feeling really lazy, we just scavenge a picnic from what's in the fridge and then cozy up for a movie, or catch up with some of our favorite TV series.”

—Daphne

“**TO ME, AND MAYBE TO MOST PEOPLE,** Sunday supper means the stuff that Grandma makes. I think grandma food is pretty much what we mean when we say comfort food, because grandmas make us comfortable. In my family, we used to have at least two different meats, corn bread, homemade rolls, and no less than five sides. Grandma's house was the original all-you-can-eat buffet. Now we still love old-timey things as simple as meatloaf, mashed potatoes, and peas for Sunday dinner. Or something long braised (so you can nap and not worry about ruining dinner if you catch a few extra *z*'s). A lot of my Sunday cooking is “dump and roll,” as in you dump it in a pot and when it's done you roll it out on your plate.”

—Carla

BATTLE OF THE IRON GRANDMAS

"When it's time for the ultimate Sunday dinner, who're you gonna turn to? Grandma! So, are you rarin' to roast, stoked to sauté, burstin' to braise? Get ready for the greatest throwdown in the history of food competition: *The Chew's* Battle of the Iron Grandmas. They've had kids, changed diapers, packed school lunches, driven to music lessons, cheered their lungs out at Little League, and come home every night to cook. These are veterans of victuals, grand dames of dining, and the greatest mealtime mommas ever, ready to compete for the coveted Iron Casserole.

And not only do we have Iron Grandmas—with their very own Iron Sous Chefs Mario Batali, Michael Symon, and Carla Hall—we also have Iron Judges: Lidia Bastianich (who is an Iron Chef and a grandma), Geoffrey Zakarian, and Masaharu Morimoto.

Okay, first up, Mama T, aka the Spicy Staten Islander. Mama T, our reigning champion grandma, what do you have for us?"

—Clinton

MAMA T: I got a sausage and beef cassoulet. In Staten Island, we're happy to call it a regular old casserole. Great with a glass of wine . . . mmm . . . mmm . . . good!

CLINTON: Next up, the Sassy Southerner, Daisy the Dumpling Queen. The question on everyone's mind: Will the newcomer's dumplings dump the other mega matriarchs?

DAISY: You better believe it. It sticks to your ribs.

CLINTON: Say no more, I'm there! And over here, completing our holy trinity, Michael is working with Nona Arrabiata, the one and only Antoinette Lordo. What have you got for us?

ANTOINETTE: My sister Mary's melts-in-your-mouth meatloaf. I'm not a big meatloaf fan.

CLINTON: Don't oversell it, Antoinette.

ANTOINETTE: Yeah, but this meatloaf, fuggedaboutit!

CLINTON: Okay, may the best grandma win.

OKAY, JUDGES, time to chop some grandmas. And, audience, I have to tell you, it's a rare thing in the cooking-competition world that Chef Zakarian joined the Clean Plate Club with Mama T, Lidia chowed down on chicken and dumplings like she came from Alabama instead of Istria, and Morimoto, of the exquisite presentations and the teeny, tiny tweezer food, actually ate Antoinette's meatloaf with the pleasure he usually reserves for sea urchin custard. So this one is going to be hard.

Decision time, grandmas.

(Sound effect of clock ticking and suspense music, like in Psycho*)*

And which grandma will be taking home the golden casserole?

(Opens envelope)

AND THE WINNER IS . . . DAISY. You go home with the coveted Iron Casserole. But not to worry, our runner-up grandmas get a consolation Granny Swag Basket, complete with knitting needles, fuzzy slippers, and a mah-jongg set.

Grandmas everywhere, we learn from you, we love you, we want seconds! And, audience, try these recipes and you be the judge.

Antoinette and Mama T await the judges' decision.

Daisy's Chicken and Dumplings

SERVES 6 | COOK TIME: 35–45 MINUTES | PREP TIME: 30 MINUTES | COST: $

FOR THE CHICKEN

6 chicken legs (with or without skin)

6 chicken thighs (with or without skin)

1 tablespoon chicken seasoning

½ teaspoon lemon pepper

1 teaspoon garlic powder

½ tablespoon soul seasoning

Salt, to taste

2 tablespoons vegetable oil

2 stalks celery, chopped

1 small onion, chopped

3 liters chicken stock

FOR THE DUMPLINGS

2 cups self-rising flour

⅓ cup pancake mix

1 teaspoon seasoning salt

½ teaspoon onion powder

½ cup water

⅓ cup Carnation evaporated milk

2 teaspoons vegetable oil

2–3 ice cubes

TO MAKE THE CHICKEN

1. Season the chicken legs and thighs with the chicken seasoning, lemon pepper, garlic powder, soul seasoning, and salt. Prick the chicken all over with a fork to let the seasoning absorb.

2. Place 2 tablespoons of vegetable oil in a heavy-bottomed pot over medium-high heat, and sear the chicken, about 3 minutes per side. Once browned on all sides, add the celery and onion. Add about 3 liters of chicken stock, or enough to cover (about half a finger above the chicken). Bring to a boil and then reduce to a simmer. Cook for 20 minutes, or until the chicken is fully cooked.

TO MAKE THE DUMPLINGS

3. In a medium-sized bowl, add the flour, pancake mix, seasoning salt, and onion powder, and stir in the water, evaporated milk, vegetable oil, and ice cubes. The batter should be medium thick.

4. Use a soup spoon to help shape the dumplings. Start adding the dumplings to the pot of boiling chicken once the chicken is cooked through. Cover the pot and let boil for 1–2 minutes.

5. Remove from the heat and serve hot.

Carla and Daisy talk up their classic Southern cooking.

Mama T's Sausage and Beef Casserole

Easy

SERVES 6 | COOK TIME: 1 HOUR 15 MINUTES | PREP TIME: 20 MINUTES | COST: $

2 tablespoons vegetable oil

1 pound beef chuck, cubed (like stew meat)

1 pound sweet Italian sausage links

1 large onion, sliced

4 cloves garlic, minced

2 red or yellow bell peppers, sliced

2 14-ounce cans kidney beans, drained and rinsed

4 russet potatoes, peeled, cut in half lengthwise, and then sliced into eighths

Salt, to taste

Pepper, to taste

Dried basil, to taste

1 cup beef stock

1. Preheat the oven to 350 °F.

2. Place vegetable oil in a large cast-iron skillet over medium-high heat, brown the beef, and set aside. In the same pan, cook the sausage, breaking it up as you cook (leaving big chunks, not crumbled), and set aside. Add the onion, garlic, and bell peppers, and cook until just tender.

3. In a large casserole dish, mix together the beef, sausage, and onion mixture. Add the kidney beans and potatoes. Season with salt, pepper, and basil to taste. Add the beef stock. Mix until everything is evenly distributed.

4. Cover and bake for about 1 hour, or until the potatoes are fork tender.

No one is tougher than Team Mama T!

Moderate

Antoinette Lordo's Melt-in-Your-Mouth Meatloaf

SERVES 10 | COOK TIME: 1 HOUR 10 MINUTES | PREP TIME: 30 MINUTES | COST: $

FOR THE MEATLOAF

1 large Idaho potato

1 large onion

2 tablespoons olive oil, plus more for the pan and meatloaf

Salt, to taste

Pepper, to taste

2 pounds chuck chop meat

2 cups bread crumb flakes

½ cup grated Pecorino Romano

2 eggs

4 ounces tomato sauce

1 teaspoon parsley flakes

1 teaspoon basil flakes

1 teaspoon garlic powder

8 ounces mozzarella, cubed

FOR THE GRAVY

2 cups beef broth

Salt

Pepper

3 tablespoons corn starch

1 teaspoon gravy master

1 teaspoon onion powder

1 teaspoon brewed black coffee

½ teaspoon parsley

TO MAKE THE MEATLOAF

1. Grate the potato and onion using a box grater. Heat a large frying pan with 2 tablespoons of the olive oil. Add the grated potato and onion, season with salt and pepper, then sauté until light brown, about 5–6 minutes. Set aside and allow to cool.

2. Preheat the oven to 375 °F.

3. In a large bowl, mix the meat, bread crumbs, grated cheese, eggs, tomato sauce, parsley, basil, and garlic powder. Add the cooled potato and onion mixture, and mix well with your hands.

4. Transfer the mixture onto waxed paper and flatten into a rectangle. Lay the cubed mozzarella in the middle of the loaf and fold over all sides to cover. Transfer into a greased pan, rub the meatloaf with olive oil, and bake in the oven for 1 hour, uncovered.

TO MAKE THE GRAVY

5. Heat all the ingredients in a saucepan, stirring often until it starts to boil. Continue to stir until the mixture thickens to the preferred consistency. Serve over the meatloaf.

Antoinette flexes her best cooking muscles for the competition.

Spiked Iced Tea

SERVES 4-6 | COOK TIME: 5 MINUTES | PREP TIME: 10 MINUTES | COST: $

Easy

Mario is right that beer is an amazing thirst-quencher, but so is iced tea—especially my iced tea. The way I look at it, any recipe that calls for a whole bottle of rum has a great party attitude. The orange or lemon garnish is optional. The rum isn't.

- 1 gallon black tea, brewed
- 5 cups spiced rum
- Juice of 4 lemons, peel of one
- Juice of 4 oranges, peel of 1
- 1 orange, thinly sliced
- 1 lemon, thinly sliced
- Ice

1. Brew a gallon of black iced tea with the peels of 1 orange and 1 lemon.
2. In a large, 2½-gallon drink dispenser, add cooled iced tea, rum, lemon juice, and orange juice.
3. Add the orange and lemon slices and stir well. Fill with ice and serve.

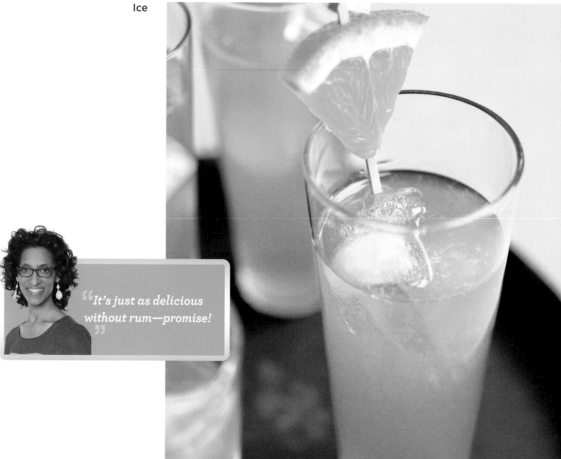

"It's just as delicious without rum—promise!"

Thai Chopped Chicken Salad

SERVES 4 TO 6 | PREP TIME: 20 MINUTES | COST: $

Easy

Most of us think when we order something called "salad" that automatically means we are really eating healthfully. Think twice. Caesar salad can have 700–800 calories. A normal serving of chicken salad is 600 calories, but this light salad, made with leftover roast chicken, is hundreds less. It's also loaded with super flavorful ingredients like mangoes and soy sauce and rice vinegar, proving that healthy doesn't have to mean boring. And when you get the calorie bill, it's about half of regular chicken salad at the deli or sandwich shop. This salad is a perfect two-fer when you use leftover roast chicken from the Roast Chicken with Salsa Verde and Creamy Potatoes recipe on page 212.

- 4 cups roast chicken, shredded
- 1 mango, peeled and diced
- 1 cup snow peas, thinly sliced
- Scallion (green and white parts), sliced
- ⅓ cup olive oil
- 1 Fresno chili, seeded and minced
- 1 clove garlic, minced
- 1 tablespoon honey
- 2 tablespoons light soy sauce
- 2 tablespoons rice vinegar
- 1 head Bibb Lettuce, whole leaves separated, to serve
- ¼ cup peanuts, chopped, to garnish
- Salt, to taste
- Freshly ground pepper, to taste

1. Combine the chicken, mango, snow peas, and scallion in a bowl. In another bowl, whisk the olive oil, Fresno chili, garlic, honey, soy sauce, and rice vinegar together. Pour the dressing over the chicken mix and toss to coat. Spoon into the lettuce cups and garnish with the peanuts. Season to taste.

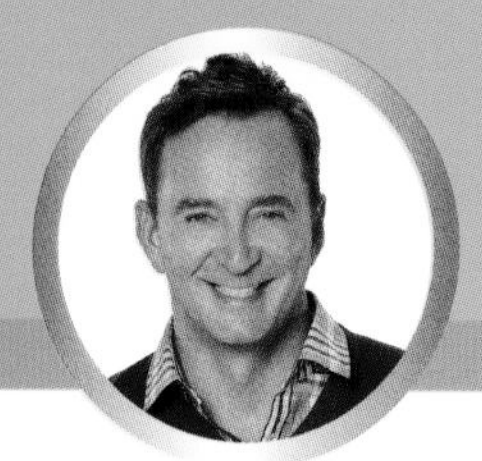

Roast Chicken with Salsa Verde and Creamy Potatoes

2 FER

SERVES 6 | COOK TIME: 50–55 MINUTES | PREP TIME: 30 MINUTES | COST: $$

Easy

You've heard of steak and potatoes guys. Well, that's fine, but I'm also a chicken and potatoes guy. Really one of the measures of a chef is how well he or she makes a roast chicken. Make this one, and you'll measure up. Mine is a bunch of "nots," as in I do not brine it, and I don't stuff anything under the skin. I just put some lemon and sage inside, and oil and butter and seasoning on the outside, and let a good chicken basically cook itself. I love it with this salsa verde, which is kind of a spicy pesto made with a mix of herbs and some anchovy. That's the Michael Symon secret ingredient in a lot of his recipes, and if you do it right, it pumps the flavor big-time and no one is going to say, "Hey, Clinton, what's with the anchovies?" If they don't ask, I'm not gonna tell.

FOR THE ROAST CHICKEN

- 1 3-pound chicken
- Salt, to taste
- Pepper, to taste
- 2 lemons, halved
- 4–5 sage leaves
- 2 tablespoons extra virgin olive oil

FOR THE SALSA VERDE

- ¼ cup flat-leaf parsley
- 2 tablespoons mint
- ¼ cup tarragon
- 2 anchovy fillets, rinsed
- 1 clove garlic
- 1 tablespoon red wine vinegar
- Juice of 1 lemon

TO MAKE THE ROAST CHICKEN

1. Preheat the oven to 425 °F.

2. Remove the gizzard, heart, neck, and liver from the chicken, and then rinse it under cool water. Pat dry and then season the cavity with salt and pepper. Then stuff with the halved lemons and sage. Rub the olive oil all over the chicken, then, after washing your hands, generously season the chicken with salt and pepper.

3. Place the chicken on a rack in a roasting pan (or create a rack out of celery and carrots). Cook the chicken for 20 minutes in the oven, then reduce the heat to 325 °F and cook for 15 minutes per pound (approximately 30–45 minutes).

4. Remove the chicken from the oven and let rest at least 15 minutes.

5. While the chicken is cooking, make the salsa verde and potatoes.

1 shallot, chopped

2 tablespoons capers

1 teaspoon red chili flakes

½ cup extra virgin olive oil

Salt, to taste

Pepper, to taste

FOR THE CREAMY POTATOES

2 pounds russet potatoes

Salt, to taste

½–1 cup heavy cream

12 ounces butter, chilled and cubed

TO MAKE THE SALSA VERDE

6. Place all the ingredients in a food processor and pulse to combine. Adjust the seasoning with salt and pepper.

TO MAKE THE CREAMY POTATOES

7. Rub and scrub the potatoes under running water. Peel the potatoes and cut into even, large pieces. Place in a large pot and cover with cool, salted water. Bring the water to a boil, then reduce to a simmer. Cook for 15–20 minutes, or until a knife easily pierces the potatoes. Strain the potatoes.

8. In a small pot, heat the cream until scalded.

9. Using a ricer or a food mill, work the potatoes in batches over a heavy-bottomed pot. Once all the potatoes have been passed through the ricer, turn the heat on low and dry the potatoes out slightly by stirring for about 3 minutes. Stir in the butter in batches, making sure to incorporate each addition thoroughly before adding more butter. Then slowly whisk in the cream until the desired consistency. Adjust the seasoning with salt.

10. Serve the rested chicken with the salsa verde and a side of the creamy potatoes.

Swamp Thing

SERVES 6 | COOK TIME: 30 MINUTES | PREP TIME: 20 MINUTES

INACTIVE COOK TIME: 24 HOURS | COST: $

Moderate

This is my version of shrimp and grits, lightened up and without all the cheese of the traditional southern belly buster. Hey, I love it, but it doesn't love my waistline. I decided to include some of the traditional ingredients of my peeps: sweet potatoes and collards and a nice, full-flavored veggie stock. When the grits soak up all that sauce, I just want to grab my napkin and give the New Orleans version of a thumbs-up—a big old hankie wave!

FOR THE GRITS

2 cups milk

3 cups water

2 cups quick grits

1 cup fresh or frozen corn

8 tablespoons butter

Vegetable oil, for frying

FOR THE SHRIMP

3 tablespoons olive oil, plus more for the pan

1 onion, medium dice

5 cloves garlic, thinly sliced

2 carrots, medium dice

2 celery stalks, medium dice

2 cups sweet potatoes, peeled and diced

1 parsnip, peeled and diced

2 tablespoons flour

2 quarts chicken stock

4 cups collard greens, ribboned

TO MAKE THE GRITS

1. In a medium pot, heat the milk and water to a boil.

2. Slowly whisk in the grits, avoiding lumps. Cook the grits according to package time.

3. Once cooked, stir in the corn and butter until melted and incorporated.

4. Pour into a greased baking dish and allow to cool. Refrigerate overnight. Remove the grits from the refrigerator and cut into 3-inch squares.

5. Heat a nonstick pan over medium-high heat and add the vegetable oil. Fry the grits in the hot oil until golden on all sides. Remove from the pan.

TO MAKE THE SHRIMP

6. In a heavy-bottomed pot over high heat, add the olive oil. Toss in the onions and garlic, and cook for about 3 minutes.

7. Toss in the carrots, celery, sweet potatoes, and parsnip, and add more olive oil if it seems dry. Coat all the vegetables in the oil and continue to cook over high heat, just slightly browning everything.

2 teaspoons fresh thyme

1 bay leaf

½ teaspoon cayenne pepper

1 14.5-ounce can whole plum tomatoes, crushed

1 pound shrimp, peeled and deveined

Salt, to taste

Pepper, to taste

8. Sprinkle flour over the vegetables and stir. Deglaze with the chicken stock. Add the collard greens, thyme, bay leaf, and cayenne, and stir. Add in the tomatoes and bring to a boil.

9. Reduce to a simmer and cook until the vegetables are cooked through, about 15–20 minutes. Right before serving, toss in the shrimp and simmer for 2–3 minutes, or until the shrimp is just cooked through.

10. Plate in a soup bowl on top of the fried grits. Season to taste. Serve immediately.

Hold back the heat

If you want the fruitiness and some of the spiciness of a habanero chili, but not the full voltage, Bobby Flay told me to just slice the habanero and toss it in my sauce, rather than cutting it up and making the sauce super spicy.

Ham with Habanero Glaze

SERVES 10 | COOK TIME: 2½–3 HOURS | PREP TIME: 20 MINUTES | COST: $

Moderate

Many people only make fresh ham for the holidays, but it is such a super cut of pork and can easily feed any big family sit-down. I have been known to make them the way some folks might do a roast beef or leg of lamb for Sunday dinner. I like to start mine from scratch with a fresh ham that I brine with special spices and seasonings, then glaze with a tangy, spicy, sweet, and crispy habanero glaze, then super slow roast, and I make a sauce with the glaze that's my all-time favorite Cleveland Barbecue Sauce. If there is a flavor I left out of this, I'd be really surprised. It's got it all.

FOR THE BRINE

- 1 cup kosher salt
- ½ cup sugar
- 1 head garlic, halved crosswise
- 2 sprigs fresh rosemary
- 1 tablespoon black peppercorns
- 1 tablespoon coriander seeds
- 1 fresh or dried bay leaf
- 1 10-pound bone-in fresh ham (shank end)

FOR THE HABANERO GLAZE

- 1 gallon orange juice (not from concentrate)
- ½ cup fresh lime juice
- 1 habanero chili, with a slit cut in one side
- 1 cup packed light brown sugar
- 2 cups Cleveland Barbecue Sauce (recipe follows)

TO MAKE THE BRINE

1. In a large nonreactive pot over high heat, combine all the seasonings and herbs for the brine with 4 quarts of water and bring to a simmer. Whisk until the salt and sugar are completely dissolved. Remove from the heat and let cool.

2. In a container large enough to hold the ham, completely submerge the pork in the cooled brine. Weigh down the ham with a heavy plate if necessary to keep it fully submerged. Refrigerate overnight.

3. Remove the ham from the brine and pat dry with paper towels. Allow to sit out at room temperature for an hour before roasting.

4. Preheat the oven to 450 °F.

5. Score the skin, creating a diamond pattern. Transfer the ham to a roasting pan.

6. Place the ham in the oven and roast for 30 minutes to achieve a crispy skin. Reduce the heat to 350 °F and continue to roast for 1½ hours, or until the ham reaches an internal temperature of 150 °F.

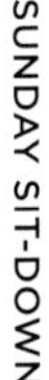

7. Baste the ham with the habanero glaze and continue to cook for 45–60 more minutes, or until the ham reaches an internal temperature of 165 °F. Remove the ham from the oven and allow it to rest for 45 minutes. Slice and serve.

TO MAKE THE HABANERO GLAZE

8. Put all the glaze ingredients in a large nonreactive saucepan over medium-high heat, and boil until reduced by half. This will take about an hour.

FOR THE CLEVELAND BARBECUE SAUCE

- 1½ teaspoons olive oil
- ½ cup red onion, minced
- 1 clove garlic, minced
- Kosher salt
- 1½ teaspoons coriander seeds
- ½ teaspoon cumin seeds
- ½ cup dark brown sugar
- ½ cup cider vinegar
- ½ cup sherry vinegar
- 1½ ounces chipotles in adobo sauce
- 1 cup stadium-style mustard (such as Bertman Ball Park Mustard)

TO MAKE THE CLEVELAND BARBECUE SAUCE

1. In a nonreactive 2-quart saucepan set over medium-low heat, heat the olive oil, onion, garlic, and a good pinch of salt. Cook until the onion is translucent, about 2 minutes. Add the coriander and cumin, and cook for 1 minute. Add the brown sugar and cook for about 2 minutes, until it melts. Add the vinegars, increase the heat to medium-high, and boil for about 10 minutes, until reduced by one-quarter. Remove from the heat.

2. Puree the chipotles in adobo sauce in a blender or food processor until smooth. Stir the chipotle puree and mustard into the barbecue sauce. Let cool. Store covered in the refrigerator for up to 3 weeks.

Italian Turkey

SERVES 6 TO 8 | COOK TIME: 3 HOURS 10 MINUTES | PREP TIME: 30 MINUTES

INACTIVE PREP TIME: 24 HOURS | COST: $

Moderate

For our Thanksgiving show, in my honor, Mario made his version of a Greek-style turkey (which would probably get him arrested in Greece), while I tried my hand at an Italian-themed turkey. I've seen some spaghetti westerns that you might call Italian-themed turkeys, but that's another question altogether. I made a paste with every Italian ingredient under the Tuscan sun and piped it under the skin of the turkey so that as it roasted, it was bathed in the essence of pancetta, garlic, herbs, citrus, and spices. Then in the cavity, I put fennel, lemon, and garlic: *molto* Symon!

FOR THE TURKEY

1 12- to 15-pound turkey, rinsed and patted dry

Salt

1 pound pancetta

10 cloves garlic, minced

Zest of 3 lemons

Zest of 1 orange

½ cup parsley, chopped

4 sprigs rosemary, chopped

2 tablespoons red pepper flakes

2 tablespoons capers, rinsed and chopped

Baste not, want not

I am not a baster. All that opening and closing the oven makes the poor turkey crazy. It doesn't know what temperature is happening! Instead I soak a cheesecloth in Italian seasonings and olive oil and lay it over the breast. The original self-baster.

TO MAKE THE TURKEY

1. The day before roasting, rinse the turkey inside and out with cold water, set on a clean kitchen towel, and pat dry. Season the turkey inside and out with the salt. Wrap the turkey in plastic wrap and refrigerate for 24 hours.

2. Remove the turkey from the refrigerator 1–2 hours prior to roasting to bring to room temperature.

3. Put the pancetta in the bowl of a food processor and pulse until it forms a paste. Transfer to a bowl and mix in the garlic, citrus zest, parsley, rosemary, red pepper flakes, and capers by hand, until thoroughly blended.

4. Place the turkey, breast side up, on a rack set into a large roasting pan. Fold the wings and tuck the tips underneath the bird.

5. Carefully put your hands underneath the turkey skin and separate the skin from the breast. Put the pancetta mixture in a piping bag, and pipe between the skin and the turkey breast, pressing to even it out.

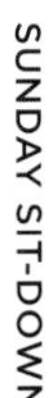

FOR THE TURKEY AROMATICS AND BASTING

- 1 head of garlic, halved through the equator
- 4 sprigs fresh oregano
- 3 sprigs thyme
- 1 lemon, quartered
- 1 onion, peeled and quartered
- 1 fennel bulb, quartered, plus ¼ cup picked fennel fronds
- 8 tablespoons olive oil
- 1 cup chicken stock (or turkey stock or water)

TO MAKE THE TURKEY AROMATICS AND BASTING

6. Preheat the oven to 425 °F.

7. In the turkey's neck cavity, place a few cloves of the garlic, a sprig of oregano, a sprig of thyme, and a quarter of the lemon. Wrap the neck skin over and around the cavity to enclose the seasoning ingredients.

8. In the body cavity, place half of the remaining garlic, half of the onion, half of the fennel, the fennel fronds, 2 lemon quarters, and half of the remaining oregano and thyme.

9. Meanwhile, in a small saucepot, combine all the remaining basting ingredients and bring to a simmer. Let cook for about 10 minutes. Remove from the heat and allow to cool slightly.

10. When cool enough to handle, soak a double layer of cheesecloth big enough to cover the bird in the basting mixture and drape it over the breast and legs of the turkey. Pour the remaining contents of the pan over the bird, pushing the pieces of vegetable and herbs into the bottom of the roasting pan. Add the neck and gizzards to the bottom of the roasting pan.

11. Place the turkey in the oven and roast for 45 minutes (there will be the distinct possibility of smoke, depending on how clean your oven is). Turn the oven temperature down to 375 °F, and continue to roast for another 15–20 minutes per pound (removing the cheesecloth for the final 10 minutes to brown, if needed), or until an instant-read thermometer inserted into the center of a thigh registers 160 °F (about 3 hours). Remove the turkey from the oven and set on a platter. Allow it to rest for 20 minutes before carving.

FOR THE GRAVY

2 links fennel sausage, removed from their casings

½ fennel bulb, finely diced

3 tablespoons flour

1 cup white wine

3 cups turkey stock, warmed

3 tablespoons butter

Salt

Pepper

TO MAKE THE GRAVY

12. Return the roasting pan to the stove and place over medium-high heat. Add the sausage and fennel, and cook until browned, about 7 minutes. Add the flour to the sausage mixture, stir in, and cook for 2–3 minutes longer. Deglaze with the wine and reduce by half. Then add in the turkey stock and bring to a simmer. Cook for a few minutes until the gravy is thickened. Whisk in the butter and adjust the seasoning.

13. Serve the gravy with the turkey.

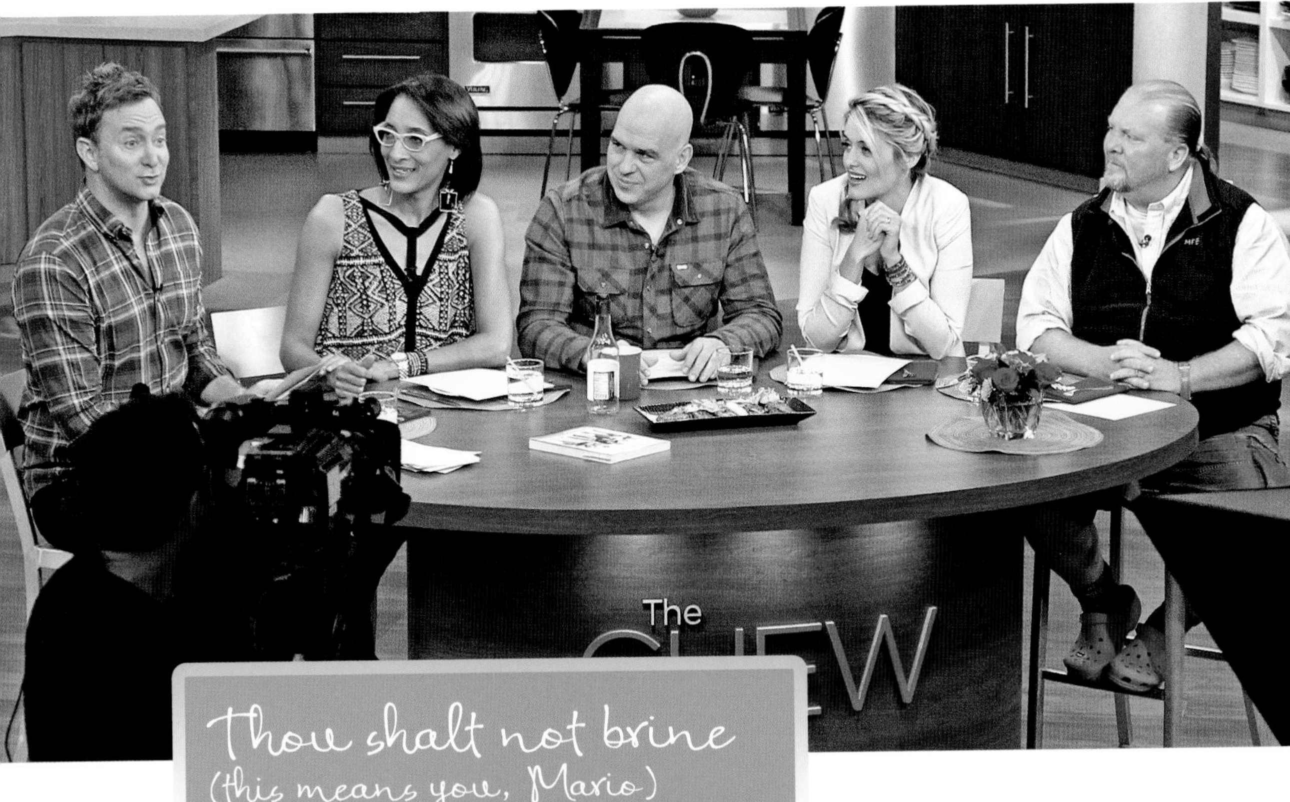

Thou shalt not brine (this means you, Mario)

Mario is a briner; I am a seasoner. I hate brining, but don't get me started. Let's just say that I think it affects the texture of the meat. Of course, that's just me. Chef Batali couldn't disagree more. That's what makes turkey races, to coin a phrase. I season mine the night before, inside and out, so the seasoning is infused into the meat.

Greek Turkey

SERVES 6 TO 8 | COOK TIME: 3–3 ½ HOURS | PREP TIME: 1 HOUR

INACTIVE PREP TIME: 12 HOURS | COST: $

Moderate

Michael, if I ever doubted, that Italian Turkey is proof that there's part of you that is pure *Italiano*, but today I am channeling the Greek part, starting with something Michael never does...a brine! And just to Greek it up a bit, I add a couple of pops of ouzo. Then, to use another non-Symon technique, I baste my turkey! Actually it's a self-baster because I put thick, creamy Greek yogurt under the skin so that it melts, moistens, and tenderizes as your bird bakes; I throw in lots of dill too. There's dill and garlic and lemon—the holy trinity of the Greek kitchen—everywhere in this recipe. In the brine, in the baste, inside the cavity, and in my avgolemono Greek gravy, based on eggs and lemons. It's all so Greek tasting that I believe even Michael would concede this turkey is perfect for partying at the Parthenon!

FOR THE TURKEY

1 gallon water

1 cup sea salt

1 bunch fresh mint

¼ cup coriander seeds, toasted, plus 1 tablespoon coriander seeds, toasted and ground

1 tablespoon dried thyme

1 bunch dill

2 cups honey

10 cloves garlic

1 gallon ice water

2 cups ouzo

1 12- to 15-pound turkey

3 bulbs roasted garlic

1 lemon, quartered

2 cups Greek yogurt

TO MAKE THE TURKEY

1. In a large stockpot, combine the water, sea salt, mint, ¼ cup coriander seeds, thyme, dill, honey, and garlic. Bring to a boil, and stir frequently to be sure the salt is dissolved. Remove from the heat and let cool to room temperature.

2. When the broth mixture is cool, pour it into a clean 5-gallon bucket. Stir in the ice water and ouzo.

3. Place the turkey, breast down, into the brine. Make sure that the cavity gets filled. Place the bucket in the refrigerator overnight but no longer than 12 hours.

4. Remove the turkey. Carefully drain off the excess brine and pat dry. Discard the excess brine.

5. Preheat the oven to 425 °F. Arrange an oven rack on the lower third of the oven.

6. Place the turkey in a roasting pan on a rack. Tuck the roasted garlic cloves in the cavity of the bird, along with the lemon.

½ cup dill, chopped

Salt, to taste

Pepper, to taste

Extra virgin olive oil

FOR THE GRAVY

2 cups chicken stock

¼ cup dill

½ cup turkey drippings

Zest of 2 lemons, plus juice of 1 lemon

8 egg yolks

Salt, to taste

Pepper, to taste

7. Mix the yogurt with the chopped dill and the remaining coriander. Season with salt and black pepper. Take your hand and loosen the skin from the breast. With a piping bag, gently distribute the yogurt mixture under the skin of the turkey, in the cavity, and on the turkey skin.

8. Drizzle the olive oil over the turkey and place it in the oven. Cook for about 30 minutes, and then reduce the oven temperature to 325 °F. Continue cooking until a thermometer reads 160 °F when inserted into the thickest part of the thigh, about 2½–3 more hours.

9. Let the turkey rest for 20–30 minutes before carving.

TO MAKE THE GRAVY

10. In a small saucepan, add the stock, dill, turkey drippings, and lemon zest and juice. Bring to a simmer and slowly whisk in the eggs. Do not boil or the eggs will scramble. Adjust the seasoning with salt and pepper.

Cheesy Bacon, Butternut Squash, Mac 'n Cheese Casserole

SERVES 6 | COOK TIME: 20–25 MINUTES | PREP TIME: 15 MINUTES | COST: $

Easy

This Sunday casserole was actually born from a fridge-raider foray to a home on Long Island. The kids told me, "Anything but string beans." I let that go in one ear and out the other. The secret to kid-friendliness is the universally beloved mac and cheese. And once you've made friends—this is your opportunity to sneak in some healthy vegetables like kale, and butternut squash, and my secret flavor picker-upper, some smoky, peppery chipotle powder.

Salt, to taste

1 pound conchigliette (pasta shells) or penne

1 pound bacon, diced

3 tablespoons butter

Pepper, to taste

1 onion, diced

1 butternut squash, peeled and diced

2 cups kale, ribbed and cut into strips

2 cloves garlic, minced

3 tablespoons flour

3 cups milk

⅓ cup half-and-half

1½ cups grated gruyere

1 teaspoon freshly grated nutmeg

½ cup mascarpone or cream cheese

1½ tablespoons chipotle powder

2 cups bread crumbs

kosher salt and freshly ground black pepper, to taste

¼ cup parsley, chopped

1. Preheat the oven on broil. Bring a pot of water to a boil and season with salt. Cook the pasta 1 minute short of the package directions.

2. In a Dutch oven, cook bacon until crisp. Add the butter to the bacon fat, then sweat the onion, butternut squash, kale, and garlic until translucent.

3. Add flour to make a roux, and slowly pour in the milk and half-and-half while mixing. Bring mixture to a simmer.

4. Stir in the butternut squash puree. Cook gently until the mixture thickens, about 4-5 minutes.

5. Add in 1 cup of the gruyere and grate in the nutmeg, and constantly stir until all of the cheese is melted. Add the mascarpone or cream cheese, and mix until melted and combined. Stir in the chipotle powder and add the cooked pasta.

6. Toss pasta until it is well mixed. Turn the broiler to high. Sprinkle the bread crumbs over the casserole. Place the Dutch oven on a rack 6 inches from the heating source. Broil for about 1 minute, or until the topping is crunchy and golden. Garnish with parsley and serve in the Dutch oven.

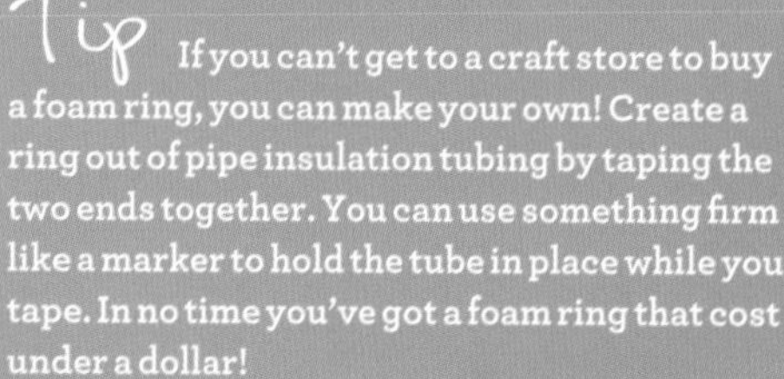

Tip If you can't get to a craft store to buy a foam ring, you can make your own! Create a ring out of pipe insulation tubing by taping the two ends together. You can use something firm like a marker to hold the tube in place while you tape. In no time you've got a foam ring that cost under a dollar!

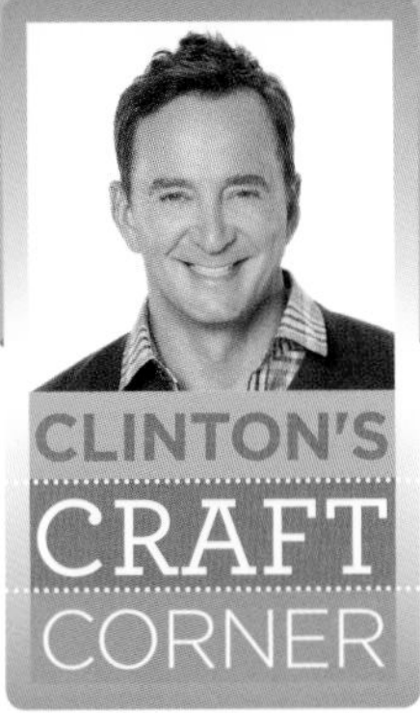

A wreath full of blessings

And now for one of the most beautiful crafty things I have ever run across. It truly looks like a painstakingly made faux floral wreath, but it's only unused coffee filters, food coloring, and some inexpensive foam piping. It takes a little time to make, but so did the needlepoint that grandmas used to do, so it seems perfect for a Sunday supper like Grandma would make. So start pinning your wreath together, and with each filter, count one of your blessings.

WHAT YOU NEED

- Large, shallow bowls
- Food coloring
- Water
- Spoons
- Coffee filters
- Paper towels
- Straight pins
- Foam ring or foam piping (see Tip)
- Ribbon

HOW TO MAKE IT

1. In the bowls, add food coloring and water, and mix with spoons. Experiment with different amounts of dye to achieve the desired color.

2. Dip coffee filters into the food-coloring mixture and lay them out to dry on paper towels.

3. Once the filters have dried, begin shaping them by pinching the middle of the coffee filter and twisting to make a flower. Put a straight pin through the base of the flower and use it to attach the flower to the ring.

4. Continue creating flowers and pinning around the ring until all of the foam is covered. String a ribbon around the wreath or add a bow for a nice accent.

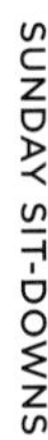

Scallion Chili Sweet Potato Cake

SERVES 6 | COOK TIME: 25 MINUTES | PREP TIME: 20 MINUTES | COST: $

Easy

This is one of those dishes that I can eat for breakfast, lunch, dinner, or even a snack. Alongside a turkey or a pork roast or a leg of lamb, it's got the flavor oomph to stand up to those major pieces of meat, but it is all light, vegetarian ingredients so it doesn't weigh you down. Take the time to crisp the layers of sweet potato on the top and bottom so you get a firm, crunchy golden-brown effect. Chili and scallions work so well in those scallion pancakes that you get in Vietnamese restaurants, I thought, "Hey, why not with sweet potatoes?" Take it from me—there is no reason why not.

FOR THE SWEET POTATO CAKE

2⅔-pounds large sweet potatoes, peeled

½ cup extra virgin olive oil

2 Fresno chilies, sliced into rounds

1 cup fresh scallions, finely chopped

Salt

Pepper

FOR THE SALAD

½ cup scallions, sliced, plus more for garnish

1 cup parsley, leaves picked

¼ cup capers

2 tablespoons balsamic vinegar

2 tablespoons olive oil

Salt

Freshly cracked black pepper

TO MAKE THE SWEET POTATO CAKE

1. Preheat the broiler to high. Arrange a rack 6 inches away from the heating source.
2. Boil the potatoes for 20 minutes, and let them cool before slicing them into ¼-inch-thick slices.
3. Heat a couple of tablespoons of olive oil in a 6- or 8-inch cast-iron pan over medium heat. Cook the Fresno chilies and scallions for a few minutes, until softened. Remove the mixture from the pan and set aside.
4. Add as many potato slices as can fit in one layer of the pan. Cook for about 3 minutes per side, or until lightly browned. Remove the pan from the heat.
5. Arrange the remaining potatoes into even layers over the crispy potatoes, seasoning with salt and pepper and some of the Fresno chilies and scallions. Press each layer down firmly with the back of a spatula or wooden spoon.
6. Cook the sweet potato cake in the oven and brown for about 3 minutes, or until the potatoes are crispy.

TO MAKE THE SALAD

7. Toss the salad ingredients together and season with salt and pepper.
8. Cut the potato cake into wedges and serve garnished with the salad and remaining scallions.

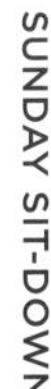

Cranberry-Apple Cobbler

SERVES 6 | COOK TIME: 1 HOUR | PREP TIME: 20 MINUTES | COST: $

Easy

This past summer, I made a cobbler every weekend until I got it perfect. No sooner were those words out of my mouth than Carla, the Dominatrix of Dessert, said, "I'll be the judge of that." The first thing you want for a perfect cobbler is perfect fruit. So get it when it's in season: blackberries, blueberries, peaches, apples, pears—they all have their peak time. Start there. For me, one of the nicest things about a cobbler is that you have all the fun of a pie, but you don't have to spend all that time on the crust. It has crisp and not crust! That's what makes it foolproof.

FOR THE COBBLER FILLING

5 Granny Smith apples, peeled and chopped

1 cup cranberries

¼ cup white sugar

¼ cup brown sugar

½ teaspoon ground cinnamon

⅛ teaspoon nutmeg

2 teaspoons cornstarch

Juice of 1 lemon

Generous pinch of salt

FOR THE COBBLER TOPPING

¾ cup milk

1 cup all-purpose flour

½ cup sugar

2 teaspoons baking soda

2 pinches of salt

8 tablespoons butter

TO MAKE THE COBBLER FILLING

1. Preheat the oven to 350 °F.

2. In a large bowl, toss together all the ingredients for the cobbler filling.

TO MAKE THE COBBLER TOPPING

3. In a separate bowl, whisk together the topping ingredients.

4. Put the butter in the pie dish and place in the oven until melted. Remove the dish from the oven and fill with the fruit mixture. Pour the cobbler topping over the fruit.

5. Bake for approximately 1 hour, or until the juices are bubbling and the cobbler is golden. Tent with foil if the cobbler is getting too brown.

Lemon Pound Cake

SERVES 6 | COOK TIME: 50–60 MINUTES | PREP TIME: 20 MINUTES | COST: $

Easy

In 1998, I was named one of *Food & Wine*'s best new chefs, which, if you do the math, makes me one of the best old-ish chefs at this point. Part of the deal—I mean honor—was that they ask you to make something at the *Food & Wine* Classic in Aspen, and even though I'm not a pastry chef, I signed up for dessert. I knew it had to be kind of a foolproof one. What could be easier than pound cake? It was kind of my coming-out party, and in this dessert you can relive my virgin voyage into big-time chef-dom. I hope you find it as thrilling as I did, or at least pretty good.

½ cup yellow cornmeal

1 cup all-purpose flour

½ teaspoon baking soda

½ teaspoon salt

3 eggs, separated

½ cup butter

1¼ cups sugar

2 tablespoons grated lemon zest, plus 6 tablespoons fresh lemon juice

½ cup milk

Lavender Simple Syrup (recipe follows)

Strawberries

TO MAKE THE CAKE

1. Preheat the oven to 350 °F. Line a 9-by-5-inch loaf pan with parchment.

2. Combine the cornmeal, flour, baking soda, and salt, and set aside.

3. Beat the egg whites until stiff and set aside.

4. Cream the butter, sugar, and lemon zest until fluffy, then add the egg yolks and mix well.

5. Add the lemon juice and then milk to the egg yolk mixture. Stir in the dry ingredients.

6. Carefully fold in the beaten egg whites, and spoon the batter into the prepared pan.

7. Bake for 50–60 minutes, or until a toothpick inserted near the center of the cake comes out clean.

8. To serve, cut slices of the cake and brush with the Lavender Simple Syrup. Top with fresh strawberries.

FOR THE LAVENDER SIMPLE SYRUP

3 sprigs lavender

1 cup sugar

1 cup hot water

TO MAKE THE LAVENDER SIMPLE SYRUP

1. Steep the lavender in the sugar and water until all the sugar dissolves. Strain out the lavender and allow the syrup to cool. Store in the refrigerator.

Grilled Pineapple Upside-Down Sandwich

SERVES 5 | COOK TIME: 5 MINUTES | PREP TIME: 10 MINUTES | COST: $

Easy

One of my all-time, all-time desserts is a pineapple upside-down cake. Even more favoriter—if I can make up a word—is when you can take something like Michael's Lemon Pound Cake on page 231 and use the leftovers. Then all you need is to make some syrup, grill some pineapple, and slather on some mascarpone cheese the way you might schmear mayo on a non-dessert sandwich.

- ½ cup butter
- ½ cup brown sugar
- ½ cup unsweetened pineapple juice
- 1 cup mascarpone
- 1 fresh pineapple, peeled, cored, and sliced
- 10 slices pound cake or challah bread
- Cherries, to garnish
- Toothpicks

1. Combine the butter, brown sugar, and pineapple juice in a pot. Bring to a boil, then reduce to a simmer for 2 minutes. Reserve half for brushing on the fresh pineapple. Mix the other half into the mascarpone.
2. Preheat a grill to medium heat. Place the pineapple rings on the grill. Grill both sides for 1 minute each, or until warmed through, then brush with the brown sugar mixture. Grill again quickly on each side.
3. Clean the grill, then quickly grill the cake. Smear each piece of cake with the sweetened mascarpone and place a grilled pineapple ring in between two slices.
4. Top with a cherry skewered with a toothpick to serve.

Stanley Tucci can hardly wait to try one of Carla's sweet treats!

Heat and sweet

Even when fruit is not totally ripe, grilling or otherwise heating develops some of those same sugars they would get in the heat of the sun.

Nectarine Blackberry Buckle

SERVES 8 | COOK TIME: 40–45 MINUTES | PREP TIME: 20 MINUTES | COST: $

Easy

Okay, to answer the question that is probably on your mind, a buckle is what you call a cross between a cake, a crumble, and a pie. It's fresh fruit in a beautiful cake batter with a crumble top. If you want to do it really old-timey (which is the best way to do anything, in my book), you bake it in a parchment-lined cast-iron skillet, just like they did back in the *Little House on the Prairie* days.

FOR THE CAKE

1½ sticks unsalted butter, plus 1 tablespoon for greasing

1½ cups all-purpose flour

2 teaspoons baking powder

¾ teaspoon salt

½ teaspoon cinnamon

½ cup sugar

½ cup light brown sugar

2 large eggs

⅔ cup buttermilk

5 nectarines, halved, pitted, and sliced

1 pint blackberries

Zest of 1 lemon

FOR THE STREUSEL

1 stick butter

¼ cup sugar

¼ cup light brown sugar

½ cup all-purpose flour

¼ teaspoon cinnamon

Pinch of salt

FOR THE WHIPPED CREAM

2 cups heavy cream

½ cup sugar

1 teaspoon vanilla

1 teaspoon cinnamon

TO MAKE THE CAKE

1. Preheat the oven to 350 °F. Line a 10-inch cast-iron skillet with parchment and grease it with 1 tablespoon of the butter.

2. Melt the remaining butter in a small saucepan over medium-low heat until light brown. Set aside to cool.

3. In a large bowl, whisk together the flour, baking powder, salt, and cinnamon.

4. In another large bowl, whisk together the cooled browned butter and sugars. Then add the eggs, one at a time. Stir in the buttermilk.

5. Add the dry ingredients into the wet. Pour the batter into the prepared pan.

6. In a large bowl, toss the nectarines and blackberries with the lemon zest and arrange them in a single layer on top of the batter.

TO MAKE THE STREUSEL

7. In a medium bowl, combine all the ingredients for the streusel. Mix together to form a crumb. Crumble over the nectarines and blackberries. Place in the oven and bake for 40–45 minutes.

TO MAKE THE WHIPPED CREAM

8. Combine the cream, sugar, and vanilla, and beat until peaks form. Fold in the cinnamon. Serve the buckle topped with whipped cream.

INDEX

INDEX